Wicked
HAMPTON COUNTY

Wicked
HAMPTON COUNTY

MICHAEL DeWITT JR.

THE
History
PRESS

Published by The History Press
Charleston, SC
www.historypress.com

Copyright © 2023 by Michael DeWitt Jr.
All rights reserved

Cover images: courtesy of the *Hampton County Guardian* archives.

First published 2023

Manufactured in the United States

ISBN 9781467153409

Library of Congress Control Number: 2022951584

This book is dedicated to the future of Hampton County: our children.
Where will you go from here?

As I am now, so you must be. Prepare for death and follow me.
—Tombstone inscription of Thomas Roberts, died March 6, 1818,
Black Swamp–area cemetery, southern Hampton County

CONTENTS

PREFACE

*P*lease allow me an introduction. I live on a small family farm in southern Hampton County. Chickens and guinea fowl peck the grounds, and herds of livestock roam nearby. It is nothing fancy, yet it sits on land gifted to my ancestors in a grant from an English king, or so the family story goes.

My family has called this place home for more than three hundred years. Sadly, one side of my ancestral tree owned vast plantation lands and numbers of enslaved persons; the other side included notorious poachers, hog rustlers and shady characters who distilled high-proof "swamp juice" under the light of the moon. Through my arteries ebb the spirits of the saintliest of southerners, muddled with the blood of generations of lawless scoundrels. Through my veins flows the essence of small-town southern America: a mixture of oppressor and oppressed, of righteous and wrongdoer. I am all that's right with Hampton County and all that's wrong with this place.

I know much about greatness and much about wickedness and scandal, and I have an appreciation for both. Perhaps that is why I became a storyteller for my community.

However, one might wonder why anyone would want to share the wicked deeds and dark secrets of his own hometown.

Edna DeLoach Sauls, or Aunt Edna, as I called her, was my grandmother's sister, one of four daughters born during the Great Depression to a Hampton County farmer and carpenter, Devie DeLoach. Devie died when I was a year old. There is a family photo of him holding me, but obviously I don't remember the man and really didn't know him. All I have of him and his generation are family stories.

When I was a child, my parents and grandparents shared wonderful family stories, tales of great men and women who did wonderful things and left behind a solid family legacy that we should be proud of.

Then Aunt Edna would share her memories, but her stories were different. She often spoke of great tragedy and wicked deeds, of men locked in battles with alcohol and their own demons and the women who loved them, stood by them and tried to make them better. While some families kept their skeletons buried in the back of the darkest closets, Aunt Edna brought them out and introduced them to me, one by one.

Perhaps there was a reason for sharing those stories and a lesson to be gleaned from her recounting of our scandalous past. Or perhaps that's just how her memory worked: she remembered the bad along with the good and then found truth somewhere in the middle.

In Aunt Edna's tales, the family heroes are no less great. But unlike the usual family stories, in which the characters gleam with an almost perfect shine in a descendant's memory, in her stories, our people seemed more real, more honest and believable, more lifelike and relatable, and definitely more interesting. She taught me that a man can have greatness in him and still have flaws—a valuable lesson for a storyteller.

I always preferred Aunt Edna's version of family history.

We live in a world of two pasts, two histories. There is the glorious, gilded version, the painted pretty side that we want the world to see, the side that we want the generations that follow to remember and judge us by. But the problem with this version of history, besides the fact that it is often exaggerated, or sometimes simply untrue, is that it is not complete, not three-dimensional. In short, it simply doesn't show the warts along with the beauty marks.

Then there is our dark, shadowy history, which is often brutal, violent and detrimental to others whose historical timelines run parallel to our own, like strains of DNA embedded within our lives that we cannot deny. No matter how ugly or unsightly this history is, it is ours to claim, to learn from, to atone for, to continue to overcome.

This book was written by a journalist and a storyteller and not just a historian. History, like journalism, should seek to tell all sides of a story and portray all sides of its characters—its heroes and its villains. No character is all good or all bad. No event or accomplishment is well received or celebrated by all. Old traditions that are celebrated by some are cursed by others. Progress, while sought by some, is resisted by others.

There is conflict here in *Wicked Hampton County*, and that is the lifeblood of any story. *Wicked Hampton County* is not a history of great deeds; libraries are fully stocked with volumes of those tomes. This is a collection of stories of great misdeeds and how one small town in America overcame them.

This is the side of our history that you won't read about in tourism brochures or county websites, but it is nonetheless our story. I think that Aunt Edna would like this version of our history.

After you read of our wicked past, know also that people can change and communities can change. Hampton County has come a long way from the days of Reconstruction, Prohibition and civil rights struggles, and it continues to evolve and grow.

When we fully acquaint ourselves with the sins of the past, the question is: Where do we go from here, Hampton County?

ACKNOWLEDGEMENTS

I gratefully acknowledge Wayne Knuckles and Martha Bee Anderson, former editors of the *Hampton County Guardian*, whose research I inherited; my wife, Valerie DeWitt, for compiling additional research; and the staff at the Hampton County Historical Society and Hampton County Library for their hospitality in granting me full access to their archives. I must also acknowledge the elders, the storytellers, the lovers of legend, the town gossips, the secret-keepers who just couldn't keep secrets. I paid attention even when you thought I wasn't listening.

1

HAMPTON COUNTY'S FIRST FAMILIES

The history of the Americas and the subsequent European exploration and colonization is a mixture of great courage and great violence, of great wealth and great wickedness. The South Carolina Lowcountry's history is no exception. Like elsewhere in the Americas, Hampton County's roots are steeped in blood.

While Eurocentric versions of history once regaled schoolchildren of my generation with tales of "discovery" and the "New World," there were civilizations of people living in the Hampton County area long before the first white man landed, and even their history is saturated with blood and driven by violence. Many of the tribes living here when European colonists arrived had fled warfare and violence from the far North or South and, once established in South Carolina, frequently warred with each other.

The Hampton County area has a rich and diverse Native American history dating back to prehistoric times. Native Americans settled and lived in this area for thousands of years, and while there are no reservations or major archaeological sites in this immediate inland region, the Native American legacy lives on in the place-names here. That legacy flows in the rivers Savannah, Coosawhatchie, Salkehatchie and Combahee. It still rides like a midnight ghost along the road we still call Pocotaligo. It lingers in places called Palachuchola and Huspah. The chert arrowheads of warriors and hunters lie hidden and buried beneath our footsteps. We are not aware of these artifacts unless the occasional spring rain or turn of a farmer's plow brings them to the light of day.

Humans thrived here for at least thirteen thousand years, from the prehistoric Paleo-Indian, Archaic, Woodland and Mississippian eras to the historic European period. Some were here when the Spanish arrived in the 1500s; others migrated north from Florida to trade or war with the English and other Europeans. The original inhabitants were a number of small tribes collectively referred to as Cusabos. They were speakers of a language called Muskhogean, the most common language in the Southeast, and they were related to the powerful Creeks in Georgia and Alabama. The most well-known tribe among them was the Yamasee, a name that once brought terror to European settlers.

While looking back over more than one hundred years of Hampton County's history for a 1978 centennial article in the *Hampton County Guardian*, award-winning editor Martha Bee Anderson described these Native Americans as "Hampton County's first families." No "wicked" history of this region would be complete without acknowledging the early people who once lived and thrived here, calling it home, before invading colonizers and explorers eventually wiped out their existence.

THE ARRIVAL OF EUROPEANS

They were our first Lowcountry families, but their days began coming to an end when Spanish explorers made treks into the region from the coast, with some explorers visiting here as early as 1521. Juan Pardo is credited with penetrating deep into what is now Hampton County in 1566, launching his party from coastal Port Royal in the Old Beaufort District.

According to Anderson's research, Native American massacres wiped out Spanish attempts at settlements in the Beaufort District, as well as a French settlement led by Jean Ribaut in 1562, which reportedly perished in a "dog-eat-dog" struggle. A settlement by Scottish Covenanters was also attempted in 1686.

Later, the English began to move into this land and settle, with the first permanent settlement dating to 1670. The English brought with them the African enslaved people needed to work the rice and cotton plantations. At first, coastal Natives were friendly with the English venturing in around 1670 and even helped protect them from the warring Spaniards.

But hostilities soon grew after disputes sparked by a Pocotaligo "Indian agent" and other unscrupulous traders grew, causing the terrible Yamasee War.

THE YAMASEE UPRISING

The Native Americans did not simply flee this area and go quietly into the night of history. Various wars ravaged this region, including a surprise uprising of Native Americans in the Yamasee War of 1715–18. Despite its name, this widespread uprising—from the Savannah River to Charleston—also included a few Cherokees, Creeks and Choctaws, although these tribes did not officially ally with one another.

Based along the Savannah, the Yamasee had built strong trade relations with the British settlers. At first, the Natives traded deerskins for European goods, but after this practice drastically depleted the local whitetail deer population, the Yamasee also began raiding Florida tribes to capture prisoners for trade as enslaved persons for the Europeans.

In what would become a common theme in European and Native American history, colonial traders took advantage of their Native allies. Unscrupulous traders began overextending credit to tribes like the Yamasee in hopes that they could later take their land when the Natives could not pay the bill. According to research published by the Hampton Museum and Visitors' Center, at one point, the Yamasee tribes of South Carolina owed European traders one hundred thousand deerskins—a debt one historian estimated would have taken the entire tribe four years or more to repay. Another historian estimated that it would take at least two years of labor from every adult male in the tribe to settle that debt.

Even an attempt at government intervention and the creation of "Indian agents" did little to stop the mistreatment of Native Americans and the conflict that would result.

By 1715, angry and bitter over the trade disputes as well as continual colonial encroachments in their territories, the Yamasee sought to settle their debts and grievances with violence and blood. On Good Friday, April 15, 1715, a group of Yamasee rebelled and killed ninety white traders and their families in the Pocotaligo Town area. According to *Yamasee War* by Michael P. Morris, one Indian agent, Thomas Nairne, was tortured to death in a process that took several days.

Not satisfied with killing just their traders and creditors, the Yamasee then began raiding plantations near the coast, killing people and livestock. The first attacks at plantations near Port Royal, which is in modern-day Beaufort County, left more than one hundred dead, but hundreds more were able to escape by sailing away on a seized smuggler's ship. Others fled to the protection of the city of Charleston, where settlers defended a perimeter around the city.

The surrounding tribes, with the exception of the Cherokee and the Lower Creek, eventually joined the Yamasee in the fray, raiding trading posts, farms and plantations from the Savannah River to the coastal area of Charleston. Elsewhere in the Southeast region, the Creeks, Choctaws, Apalachees, Saraws, Santees and Waccamaws also rose up by June 1715 and killed their trading partners.

So formidable was this alliance, some historians argue, that it could have wiped out the European colonies from the Carolinas to Virginia if the Cherokee, one of the largest tribes with a huge population in the Carolinas, would have joined their Native brethren. In fact, South Carolina came closer to eradication than any other English colony, writes Morris in his history. But the Cherokee, who lived much farther inland, had few problems with the English at the time and either refused to help the Yamasee or even took up arms against them.

So grave was the situation that Governor Charles Craven called on all white males and even a few enslaved Black people to take up arms in defense.

The turning point of the great uprising came after bloody battles in the areas of Port Royal and Salkehatchie, where the Yamasee were overwhelmed and forced to flee south of the Savannah River. Reeling but not defeated, the Yamasee and its allies experienced the final blow in 1716, when the South Carolina colonists managed to convince other Natives, such as the Lower Cherokee, to side with them in the war.

The Native resistance further weakened when neighboring colonies began sending in reinforcements to support the South Carolina military and the New England colonies began sending more war supplies to the Carolinas. Most of the bloodshed was over by April 1716, and the conflict was entirely over by 1718.

The toll on the English colonists was immense. Roughly four hundred European lives were lost. Farmers had been driven from half of the cultivated land in the colony. The property damage and livestock loss, coupled with military costs, were estimated by historians at more than 350,000 British pounds (more than $60 million today).

This deadly war resulted in the final collapse of Native American power in the southeastern area of South Carolina. Many of the defeated Natives fled to Florida, joining runaway African enslaved persons and other Natives to become part of the Seminole tribes. The South Carolina government had undisputed control over trade with the Natives, and rangers regularly patrolled the "backcountry" and the coastlines to keep the peace.

WHAT REMAINS

When the English arrived in the Carolinas around 1670, there were nearly thirty Native American tribes living in the region. Before the Old Beaufort District was divided into what is now Beaufort County and Hampton County, the northwestern sector that would become Hampton was referred to in maps of that era simply as "Indian Lands."

When the land was first subdivided in 1717, Yamasee and Creek Indians had trading posts, trails, burial grounds and ceremonial grounds throughout the pine woods and swamplands. Creeks inhabited a section of the Savannah River wetlands at a post, Palachuchola, near modern-day Stokes Bluff. In 1761, the Yuchi tribe made a home near the Salkehatchie River.

Over the next century and a half, these Native Americans would slowly move away or become victims to disease or conflict. In 1685, it is believed there were 10,000 Native Americans in South Carolina and only 1,400 European settlers. By 1715, each numbered about 5,000. By 1790, it is estimated that only 300 Natives remained while the white population had grown to roughly 140,200.

Census data notes small pockets of Native families here and there into the modern era. In the 1880 census, the total Native American population in Hampton County was reported as two individuals living in the Peeples Township. Meanwhile, that same year, the Goethe Township reported five individuals of a "peculiar" and "mixed race" of people living in the river section of this county known locally as "Old Issue."

Arrowhead display at the Hampton County Museum @ The Old Jail. *Photo by Michael M. DeWitt Jr.*

According to the 1990 census, the Native American population in Hampton County totaled six people. Other than these descendants, only the place-names and artifacts remain of the Native American legacy in Hampton County.

Native American display at the Hampton County Museum. *Photo by Michael M. DeWitt Jr.*

WANT TO LEARN MORE?

The Hampton County Museum @ The Old Jail is home to one of the most extensive Native American artifact collections in the state. Johnny Causey, a Hampton County native, has been roaming the fields, rivers and stream banks of this region since he was a young boy and donated his lifelong collection to the Hampton County Museum in 2015. Well-known archaeologist Dr. Albert C. Goodyear called this gift "one of the largest and finest collections ever donated to science and history in South Carolina." The museum is located at 702 First Street West in Hampton.

With the help of donors and grants, the Town of Hampton recently constructed a Native American Nature Trail just off US Highway 278, near where a small Native American village was once located.

2

REBELS AND RED SHIRTS

*A*mid the bitter backdrop of Reconstruction following the Civil War, Hampton County, named after a Confederate general, was founded in 1878 as a "white county," an inland solace far from "Yankee carpetbaggers" and free Blacks, states one local history.

Old wars and old ways are not forgotten here; they live on in our roadside ruins and historical markers and even in the hearts and minds of many of our older generations. During the American Revolution, when General William Moultrie was forced to retreat from Black Swamp in 1780, the British wrought "dire destruction" on Hampton County, recalls a Hampton County history, *Both Sides of the Swamp*. The year before, in May 1779, General Augustine Prévost, marching from Savannah into South Carolina, burned what is now known as Old Sheldon Church, just outside Hampton County. The church was rebuilt but heavily damaged again during the Civil War—whether by Union troops or freemen in early 1865 remains up for current scholarly debate. In the century to follow, as Lowcountry residents traveled inland toward Yemassee and Hampton County or to the coast of Beaufort, the ruins served as a frequent reminder of our violent and war-torn history.

For some here, the destruction of the Civil War will never be forgotten, and for those people, the name *William Tecumseh Sherman* is as hated and reviled today as it was in the 1860s. General Sherman's brand of "total war" touched the landscape and the people here like no other historical event, leaving behind deep hatred and resentment that festered and grew worse during Reconstruction.

The authors of *Both Sides of the Swamp* record that our forefathers experienced their "darkest hour" when Sherman made his "ruthless march to the sea" in a path that included Hampton County. "Homes were burned, pillaged, livestock and valuables stolen. The countryside was left destitute," they write. "The War Between the States completely destroyed the economic structure of this era, as Sherman in his infamous march from Atlanta to the sea, destroyed that which was the social and physical parts of this life."

"General Sherman, you see, was no respecter of value: he burned everything from chicken coops to churches."

For some people, Sherman's wreckage was a horribly practical matter. Family farmhouses and churches were burned to the ground, and crops, livestock and belongings were stolen by pillaging Yankee troops. Family records and land deeds were destroyed when local courthouses such as the one in Gillisonville were burned.

For others, it was more idealistic. It was the wanton destruction of an entire sacred way of life. For the roughly seventy years between the American Revolution and the Civil War, the more fortunate here enjoyed the "plantation type living," as stated in *Both Sides of the Swamp*. "Those whose roots grow deep know a whole way of life was wantonly destroyed."

Here is another excerpt from this history, which was published on Hampton County's tricentennial in 1970 and was authored by a Tricentennial Commission composed of many of the descendants of the county's prominent founding families. It is evident in this work, written more than one hundred years after General Robert E. Lee surrendered to the Union, that the authors still held strong feelings about "Old Glory," as they referred to the Confederacy.

> *Even worse for the proud and cultured South, however, were the days following the War called the Reconstruction period when old Beaufort District was overrun with "Yankee" soldiers, "carpetbaggers," "scalawags" and Negroes. Since the upper part of the District was largely a white populace and the lower Negro, it was believed the formation of a "white county" might bring a change in the conditions for both races. Prince William Parish, the name of the Hampton County section, was carved from the old Beaufort District.*
>
> *The only remedy possible during the Reconstruction days in S.C. seemed to be to bring the state under the control of the white voters.*

A picture of General Wade Hampton is on display at the Hampton County Museum. *Photo by Michael M. DeWitt Jr.*

That anti-Reconstruction, racist sentiment was also shared by the writers of the *Hampton County Guardian* in that era. In the August 29, 1879 issue, which was only the second edition of the paper, the *Guardian* described the end of Reconstruction as a "great revolution" that "rolled its cleaning waters over the whole state of South Carolina" to "cleanse away the filth that had there accumulated for years."

During that period, the "harpies" and "radical carpetbaggers" and "hungry hordes of camp followers" turned "our former slaves...against their best friends," the *Guardian* wrote. "Fraud, stealing, robbery and all manner of outrage were inflicted on our people," but the good citizens of Hampton County drove out these plunderers and "redeemed themselves from bondage."

During this turbulent time in the South, a leader arose, clad in a red shirt, as were his followers, to help "restore order" to South Carolina. His name was Wade Hampton III.

This rising leader was one of three generations of prominent men named Wade Hampton. Wade Hampton Sr. was a high-ranking military officer during the American Revolution and the War of 1812. Wade Hampton Jr. had been one of the wealthiest Southern plantation owners prior to the Civil War. With this background, legendary name and a great deal of ambition, General Wade Hampton III, a popular Civil War hero of many battles, set out to reclaim and restore the South Carolina that he knew and loved.

Set in a background of turmoil and unrest from Reconstruction, the election of 1876 pitted incumbent Republican governor David Chamberlain against General Hampton.

In the months leading up to the election, Governor Chamberlain sent out militia units, often composed of Black soldiers, throughout the state to coerce voters—often viciously and violently—to reelect him.

Wade Hampton's tactics weren't much different. The general traveled the state, speaking to great crowds of citizens at every turn, blasting the Republican government and promising to restore the South to its former glory and order. At every city, town and village, General Hampton was followed by companies of supporters, known as Red Shirts, who all wore red shirts as a symbol of defiance of the northern carpetbaggers who held many of the state's elected offices. On horseback and often armed, the Red Shirts used intimidation and violent rallies to drum up votes and support for their cause.

During Hampton's 1876 gubernatorial campaign, so many of his Democratic followers—many of whom were former Confederates and members of "rifle clubs"—wore the red garb that historians often refer to it as the "Red Shirt Campaign."

The election was a close one and hotly contested. When the votes were in from every county, Hampton emerged the winner on paper. But at first, Governor Chamberlain did not concede defeat. Both parties declared victory, and both accused the other of election fraud. For five months, both candidates claimed to be the rightful governor of South Carolina. Such was the confusion that two groups of people claimed to be the House of Representatives.

The matter was settled when newly elected U.S. president Rutherford Hayes took office. A Republican, Hayes nevertheless vowed to end Reconstruction, as had Wade Hampton.

On April 10, 1877, Hayes removed federal troops from South Carolina. With no federal support, Chamberlain had no choice but to step down. Hampton became governor, marking the end of the Reconstruction era

A Confederate memorial is among the Civil War displays in the Hampton County Museum. *Photo by Michael M. DeWitt Jr.*

in the Palmetto State and the beginning of more than fifty years of Democratic control.

"Hampton was finally declared governor, and from that time white citizens have managed the affairs of the commonwealth," declared *Both Sides of the Swamp*.

Hampton's name was so highly revered in Prince William Parish that in 1877 his supporters there requested, and received, permission to name the new county Hampton County in his honor.

General Hampton himself laid the cornerstone for the new Hampton County Courthouse in 1878. On that historic fall day, Hampton's Red Shirts drilled before their hero in crisp new red uniforms made especially for the occasion by southern mothers, wives and other womenfolk.

A gray Confederate uniform on display in the Military Room of the county museum. *Photo by Michael M. DeWitt Jr.*

Hampton, a third-generation plantation owner whose family once owned roughly three thousand enslaved persons, would go on to lend his name to the county seat, the town of Hampton and, later, the area's largest local school, Wade Hampton High School, one of two in the state named in his honor.

Out of war, ruin, racism, fear and hate, Hampton County was born.

WADE HAMPTON
AND THE RIOT OF 1880

*O*nce elected and officially in power, Governor Wade Hampton immediately demanded the resignation of all Republican officials elected in 1876 and ordered their offices padlocked, claiming that they won only through fraud. The South Carolina House of Representatives declared many Republican seats as "vacant" and ordered a special election. Governor Hampton would later admit that during that election the Democrats stuffed as many as five thousand ballots, according to congressional records.

The election of 1878 was no cleaner. Hampton and the Republicans implemented voting restrictions that included grandfather clauses and property requirements in majority Black counties. The Republicans even passed a law that essentially forced some Republican Black voters to walk up to twenty-five miles to vote and separated the federal and state polls so the U.S. government supervisors couldn't see and report any fraud. So much fraud was committed that in one South Carolina precinct there was a total voter count of exactly 2,500 votes above the number of registered voters.

That election was the final coffin nail for the Republican Party during Reconstruction. During that campaign, Governor Hampton was quoted in Charleston's *News and Courier* as well as the *New York Times* as saying that any race "which placed itself in opposition [to the white race]…must give way before the advancing tide and die out as the Indians have done," adding that if Black persons continued to draw "the color line" by voting against his party, "they would be drawing it for their own destructions."

Surprisingly, many of the "old guard" in the Democratic Party felt that Governor Hampton was too liberal. As governor, he nominated Black Democrats for local offices in majority Black districts, supported public education and even went so far as to open a state-funded Black college.

In early 1879, members of the state legislature nominated Hampton to the U.S. Senate, potentially to diplomatically remove him from state political power. Hampton would serve in the Senate until his 1891 loss to an ally of then governor "Pitchfork" Ben Tillman, another controversial South Carolina historical figure who would later go on to justify violence by constituents who allegedly murdered several Black citizens.

As Hampton moved into the Senate, local politics in the county named after him were just as controversial and violent as elsewhere in the state.

HAMPTON COUNTY'S BLOODY ELECTION OF 1880

Hampton County's election year of 1880 was marked one of the "liveliest" and "most interesting" in the history of the state, reported the *Hampton County Guardian* in its 125th anniversary historical edition. Those are fairly mild terms when describing an election year marked by riots, murders, an attempted jailbreak, a train wreck and even the shotgun blasting of a politically unaffiliated mule.

Hampton County started that election year off with a daylong festival on February 26, 1880. There was a regimental review and parade by the Hampton Regiment of the South Carolina Cavalry, all clad in red shirts and Confederate uniforms, numbering in the hundreds from every corner of the county. Local politicians gave great speeches extolling the greatness of the young county and plans for the upcoming elections.

Around 2:30 p.m., the crowd learned that a disagreement on the ground-floor hall of the courthouse had resulted in the stabbing death of one man and the arrest for murder of another. Surprisingly, this did not end the action of the day.

Throughout the afternoon, there was much political and social discussion, and the two barrooms on Main Street were overflowing. By 5:00 p.m., the situation at the Courthouse Square was labeled "a formidable riot," stated the *Guardian*. During an attempt to break up the crowd, Sheriff A.M. Ruth was run from the square by pistol fire. He organized a posse that went to arrest the drunken rioters. Ruth and his posse did succeed in quieting the crowd, but only after a short battle.

The Hampton County Courthouse as it was pictured in the early 1900s. *Courtesy of the* Hampton County Guardian *archives.*

Only one person was reported as "seriously injured," but there were other reports of "broken bones, cuts and so forth."

As a result of the riot in February, by April, the newly elected Hampton town government passed an ordinance that prohibited the carrying of concealed weapons on the streets of the county seat. Reports are that this ordinance generally went unheeded.

Party conventions were held throughout the spring and summer in preparation for Election Day. The Democrats held their convention at the county courthouse, where they elected officers to attend the state party convention and planned their strategy.

The Republicans, called "Radicals" by their opponents and the *Guardian*, held their convention outside the county at Coosawhatchie in conjunction with the Beaufort County Republican Party. The Republicans continued to campaign to keep their forces from joining the Democrats as many had done in the proceeding campaigns when Wade Hampton had run for governor. They utterly denounced the policies of the Democrats. At a September campaign rally at Almeda, not far from Varnville, a Republican speaker told a large group of local Black citizens that they would all lose their voting rights if the Democrats won.

The state Democrats countered those tactics by organizing a train tour of the state, spending a day in each county.

Soon, the Republicans would strike.

The Democratic campaign day for Hampton County was set for October 18, 1880. Lots of folks were coming into town. On the night before the rally, the train engineer bringing candidates and supporters into Hampton noticed that the tracks had been sabotaged three miles below Brunson. He applied down brakes but could not stop the train completely. The engine and the express and baggage cars were all ditched, and the mail car caught fire. Fortunately for the passengers, no one was injured.

The Democrats were outraged by this incident. At the Courthouse Square the next day, there assembled six hundred mounted Red Shirts and two thousand other angry supporters. The rally was filled with emotional speeches and was "as wonderful as any produced in the state that year," reported the *Guardian*.

The Hampton County Republicans' campaign day was on October 23, 1880, at Brunson. After the train incident the week before, the Republicans were prepared for a disruption of their rally. They came "armed with pistols and loaded down with cartridges."

There was an assemblage of more than 1,500 people that day in the small village of Brunson, including all the Republicans who "could be borrowed from Barnwell, Colleton, and Beaufort counties." The meeting ended with much "whooping, yelling and firing of pistols," not unlike the Democratic event the week before.

Election Day was close at hand, but the bloodshed was far from over.

Election Day morning began with prisoners at the county jail attempting a breakout by removing a brick wall. They were caught before they finished the job, however.

There were reports of attempts by both parties to prevent people from voting in the election, as well as reports that multiple votes were "bought with whiskey." The accusations caused a tense situation in the county throughout the day. Both parties complained of election irregularities, even though the Republicans didn't even have a slate in the local county ticket.

But the most troubling reports involved gunfire and murder. In Lawtonville, near modern-day Estill, voter Isaac Colson was ambushed and shot dead on his way home from the polls. Even his mule was killed, riddled with buckshot. Contemporary literary scholars have argued that no good southern fiction is complete without at least one dead mule in the story. The same tenet must hold true for southern nonfiction.

As the polls were closing in Varnville, about one hundred Republicans converged on the polling place and began firing off pistols and other weapons. Confident of victory, the Hampton County Democrats did not bother to retaliate.

The returns of the bloody election of 1880 were received somewhat skeptically, as Hampton County reported an exact, even 1,500-vote majority for the Democratic ticket.

On a broader level, this election marked a time that would become known in U.S. history as the emergence of the "Solid South," as all southern states would vote as a Democratic bloc until 1920 and racist Jim Crow laws would become rampant.

MOONSHINE, SUE CAT AND OTHER DEMON BREWS

By the will of the people of this town, recently expressed at the ballot box, the dry schedule went into effect on Monday, Jan. 1.
—Hampton County Guardian, *1883*

Murder and mean liquor—they go together in logical order….Are conditions so much worse in Hampton County than elsewhere? Or is it that Hampton County bootleggers are somewhat dumb and stupid and get themselves caught—or that the particular kind of liquor that Hampton County bootleggers make is peculiarly conducive to criminality?
—Editorial in the Hampton County Guardian, *July 28, 1929,*
after a year with a high murder count, followed by the news of several citizens caught in a Prohibition dragnet.

Many people have the misconception that illegal alcohol and "moonshining" existed primarily during the era of national Prohibition brought on by the Eighteenth Amendment (1920–33). Nothing could be further from the truth in Hampton County and other parts of South Carolina. Contraband whiskey—more commonly called illicit liquor, bootleg, hooch or moonshine in the headlines of the day—was a political, social and religious issue for more than one hundred years. Even when alcohol wasn't outlawed at the national level, many states and counties took it upon themselves to inflict a "dry schedule" on their citizens. Such was the anti-drinking attitude of many people in that era that in March 1916 one newly elected Town of Hampton official, Intendant J.W. Vincent, described townsfolk who sold and consumed alcohol as "liquor heads" (similar to the term *potheads* widely used in the 1960s and '70s) and promised to keep the town "law abiding."

Even when alcohol was legal, states like South Carolina passed a multitude of laws to restrict or limit its use, from the "one gallon" liquor transportation restriction of 1915 to the "quart a month" bill signed into law by the governor in 1917. This law prohibited any whiskies from being imported for beverages and required an oath be made before a probate judge that the imported liquor order was for "medicinal purposes" only—reminiscent of the medical marijuana laws in some states today. This law also prohibited most women, students and minors from receiving shipments of liquor, but it was kinder to men and did show a little mercy for faithful and devout Christians. Church congregations could obtain one gallon of wine each month for religious purposes. Another law, passed in March 1933, limited the strength of beer to 3.2 percent alcohol.

Then there were the "Blue Laws," which prohibited the sale of strong drink on Sundays and on certain hours and holidays, including Election Days. Some blue laws also prohibited all types of non-alcohol-related businesses from opening on Sundays. At one point in Hampton County's history, people couldn't even legally buy a newspaper or watch a movie on the Sabbath!

Alcohol didn't become a contentious issue until after the Civil War. During Reconstruction, the victorious Union government divided the South into military districts and began enforcing new federal taxes, including exorbitant excise taxes on liquor, to help repay the war debt. A southern man could buy a gallon of whiskey for only twenty-five cents prior to the war, but now he had to buy the whiskey and then pay as much as ten times that amount in taxes. To make matters worse, the feds would often send in former Union soldiers as marshals to enforce these taxes and collect these fees, which didn't sit right with the vanquished Confederate drinking man, as you can imagine. Federal revenue officers were sometimes met with hostility and even violence, and local juries would often refuse to convict violators. Faced with these challenges, whiskey makers of that era were forced to invest big in order to go legit—or go underground and operate illegally.

After Reconstruction, the alcohol business in South Carolina was monitored by a government agency commonly called "the Dispensary." The Dispensary system of South Carolina functioned from 1892 to 1907, during which time the state had an absolute monopoly on the wholesale

Miles B. McSweeney, the founder of the *Hampton County Guardian*, went on to serve as governor of South Carolina. *Courtesy of the* Hampton County Guardian *archives.*

and retail liquor business within its borders—or so it thought. Alcohol was a central focus in the elections of 1892 and 1900, both in Hampton County and statewide, and a major issue in these elections was the Dispensary-prohibition question. This was an emotional issue that divided families, communities and political parties. Many felt that allowing the sale of liquor was a "crime against humanity," wrote the *Guardian*. Others just felt powerfully thirsty and objected strongly to government intervention in their drinking habits.

Of the thirty-five counties in the state at the time, Hampton County was one of only eight to vote "wet," or against prohibition, in 1892. Miles B. McSweeney, founder of the *Hampton County Guardian*, ran for governor on a pro-Dispensary platform and won in 1900. The *Guardian* reported that the women of the area made a "big showing" at a "Ladies Day in Hampton" prohibition rally, but since they couldn't vote, it was their thirsty husbands, fathers and brothers who carried the election.

Like many government agencies of its era, the Dispensary was known for public corruption and graft. Then along came the national Progressive movement, which wanted to tackle social issues and take on such evils as child labor while working for better workers' rights, civil rights and education. But the Progressives, led by churches and prominent "model citizens," also wanted to curb crime and public drunkenness and clean up the government, and the movement's leaders felt that shutting down agencies like the Dispensary and taking a drink out of a man's hand was the way to accomplish all of these things. At the same time, banning alcohol also became the primary goal of the national temperance movement, which was led by local women's groups that preached that alcohol was an evil in society and in the home.

Faced with the momentum of these national movements, the dispensary was closed in 1907. Within a couple of years, almost half of South Carolina's counties banned alcohol or went "dry." Then, in 1915, a statewide referendum made the manufacture, sale or enjoyment of alcohol illegal everywhere in the Palmetto State.

Those were dark days indeed for the drinking man in South Carolina.

THE BOOTLEGGER IS BORN

Then along came the local bootlegger (so named because small bottles of contraband alcohol were often hidden in a man's tall boots), who made corn liquor in dark corners of the swamp under "the shine of the moon" (thus the term *moonshiner*). "Rumrunners" would also bring in foreign booze through South's Carolina's many waterways, and Caribbean rum or scotch from the old country was often cut with local moonshine or sold straight.

These prohibition laws turned a lot of law-abiding citizens into criminals overnight. In the Palmetto State, particularly places like rural Hampton County, the moonshine business thrived from the 1860s well into the 1960s. But it was a peculiar business, one in which the wealthy often indulged in the forbidden fruit of homemade whiskey while punishing the blue-collar folks who made it. Many prominent doctors, bankers, attorneys, prosecutors, judges and law-enforcement officers enjoyed a good drink now and then while sending more than one moonshiner to court and then jail, said one elderly Hampton County man who grew up in a family that included a few moonshiners.

In a 2022 interview with the author, the late Charles Moore, then seventy-four, of Hampton, recalled his childhood experiences with the moonshiners in his family, but out of respect for his family members he declined to name the bootleggers or their well-known customers.

One of his older male relatives was arrested and prosecuted on multiple occasions by some of the same officials who bought corn liquor from him. "There were times when they would arrest him just to make it look good, I reckon," said Moore. "[He] spent more than two or three times in jail, for weeks at a time."

One of his family bootleggers rammed his vehicle into a police car while trying to escape and got a month or so in the county jail, Moore recalled. Another family 'shiner actually shot a "revenue man," blowing part of the officer's arm off, and spent a longer stretch in state prison.

Moore recalled as an eleven-year-old boy being sent to fetch the whiskey for a sale when the older men were in jail. The customers would usually come late in the evening or at night. The corn liquor, bottled in pints and quarts, would be in a cloth sack hidden deep in a head-high cornfield, along a certain numbered row, and a female relative kept the money in what he described as an "old timey bank bag."

Moore was taken, just once, to visit one of the liquor stills, which was located roughly a half-mile deep into a wooded area near the "Crosby

Hill" community and what is now part of Lake Warren State Park in central Hampton County. Moore remembers that the still was tucked away in a low-lying, fenced-in area that was a drop-off near the lake. By their clandestine nature, moonshine stills needed to be hidden and located near water sources, with thick tree cover overhead to help conceal any telltale signs of smoke or steam.

"There was a natural spring there, and you couldn't see the sky because the trees formed kind of an umbrella," described Moore. "It was well hidden—you would have to accidentally walk up on it to find it."

While sordid stories have long been told of "rot gut" moonshine that could kill you or make you go blind—where unscrupulous bootleggers would use toxic lead equipment or throw dead animals into the corn "mash" to help it ferment faster—Moore said if animals got into his family's moonshine mash it was purely by accident.

"There were times you had to pull rats or possums out of the mash," Moore said. "You couldn't close it up, or the drums would blow up."

For Moore's relatives, mostly farmers, making moonshine was simply a way to pay the bills, feed the family and keep the proverbial wolf away from the door, especially during hard economic times. Turning corn into mash and moonshine brought more money than selling a bushel of raw corn on the farmers' market.

"In those days, that's all they had to survive on," said Moore. "That was the only income that was coming in at the time."

"But they didn't sell it to children or teenagers," he added. "Only adults, including some prominent, well-respected people in the community."

In 1933, national Prohibition ended with the repeal of the Eighteenth Amendment, but some states and counties continued their dry policies. Even when it became legal again, 'shiners and corn farmers had grown accustomed to making this clandestine, tax-free income, and they depended on it. So many kept at it.

While Hampton County did not earn the reputation of other South Carolina moonshine hot spots—such as Hell Hole Swamp, where "the stills sprang up like mushrooms," or Dark Corner, where the stills were "as thick as fleas in a hog pen"—there was a thriving liquor trade here and a zealous effort by the law and elected officials to shut them down. While liquor stills could be found in almost every corner of the county, they were especially active up and down the Savannah and Salkehatchie River basin areas. One section of Hampton County, northeast of Hampton and Varnville and near the Salkehatchie swamp, was sometimes called "Liquor-ville" and was the subject of record-breaking raids. One whiskey bust on March 21, 1956, netted sixty barrels in seven stills and three thousand gallons of mash— but no arrests. "Apparently informers kept them warned in advance so they could get away," the raiding officers told the local paper.

Moonshining in those areas was often a family business, with everyone, even the children, getting involved. The April 17, 1929, issue of the *Guardian* described how certain bootleggers north of Hampton had a security system that involved either fleet-footed children or "well-trained wives." When the lawmen passed the house headed toward the woods or swamp, either a child would run and warn the bootlegger, or, if there wasn't enough time, the wife would fire a gun into the air.

To deal with this ongoing legal problem, town, county, state and even federal law-enforcement agents teamed up on raids throughout the state. Sometimes, arrested suspects would face local charges before a county magistrate, and local court dockets were often full of illegal liquor cases. In the October 1939 session of Hampton County General Sessions Court alone, eighteen guilty pleas were offered for liquor violations. In addition to the countless local charges, other cases were often sent to federal courts in Charleston or Augusta, Georgia.

For more than a century, the pages of the *Hampton County Guardian* were sprinkled with colorful front-page headlines of "illicit" liquor still raids. Stories like this one from March 7, 1928, were common:

> *Corn Whiskey Flows When Stills Busted*
> *Thousands of gallons of beer and good old corn whiskey literally flowed in Hampton County last week, when Sheriff Thomas, Deputy Sheriff Gooding, and three federal prohibition officers destroyed eleven stills throughout the county. Close to five thousand gallons of beer and corn whiskey were poured out, 98 fermenters and other still machinery were destroyed, representing a value of more than $2,100.*

Judging from the fact that the reporter wrote "good old corn whiskey," emotions and opinions on alcohol must have been mixed, even among the paper's editorial staff of that day.

While many 'shiners were otherwise peaceful, law-abiding folks, the illegal business also attracted its share of rough men who were not opposed to violence to protect their interests and stay out of jail. Local stories abound of moonshiners hurting and killing those who interfered in their trade or resisting capture by the police with violence or extreme measures. Some bootleggers used dangerous booby traps to protect their secret liquor lairs, and it was not uncommon for violators to have guns in their possession when arrested, ready to use them.

Moonshiners would go to great lengths to manufacture and deliver their product while evading detection or capture. In March 1919, a Varnville man described as a "whiskey still artist" was arrested for operating a whiskey still in his bedroom.

During the 1950s and '60s, the South Carolina Law Enforcement Division (SLED) began using aircraft to detect possible liquor manufacturing sites, often searching for something as simple as signs of smoke or steam in isolated areas along waterways.

While the cops took to the air, the moonshine men went underground—and even underwater.

A December 14, 1966, headline in the *Guardian* read, "Bootleggers Go Underwater with 'Submarine' Still." The article reported that two agents from the U.S. Alcohol, Tobacco Tax Division in Beaufort, along with county and state police, had discovered a liquor still that was "built like a submarine" deep in the Salkehatchie swamp near the Cherry Grove community, where Hampton, Allendale, Colleton and Beaufort Counties come together.

The officers watched the still "around the clock" from Thursday to Sunday afternoon that prior week and reported that it was going "full blast." On Sunday evening, they quietly rowed in by swamp boats to make the raid and arrest a pair of men who were caught unloading from a swamp boat into a car sixty-seven gallons of "swamp-hole juice" at a boat landing near the still.

As officers closed in to make the arrests, one of the moonshiners dove into the almost-icy Salkehatchie River and swam away. He evaded capture, the officers reported, because it was too cold for them to jump in and swim after him. Officers put out a four-county search for the frigid fugitive.

The officers described the submarine still as being built on a rectangular box with a conning-type tower and was accessible only by boat. It could produce twenty-five gallons of bootleg per day.

Despite its ingenious concept and design, the still was destroyed by dynamite. The car and boat were confiscated, and six hundred gallons of mash were dumped into the swamp.

MODERN-DAY MOONSHINE

When national Prohibition was lifted in 1933, wine and 3.2 percent beer could be sold again in Hampton County. Some merchants still refused to sell it. According to the April 19 issue of the *Guardian*: "Somehow there seemed to linger about the new beer and wine the aroma of illegality, as far as the personal consciences of some merchants were concerned. Others were getting ready to dispense it without delay."

On January 18, 1939, amid almost weekly reports of liquor still raids by Hampton County deputy sheriffs, the *Guardian* published a story highlighting a bill brought before the South Carolina House of Representatives to legalize the sale of alcohol and put the money in the state treasury. The story was titled, "A Dangerous Proposal."

When legal liquor finally returned to South Carolina, the local paper reported in 1935 that Hampton County was the only county in the state without a liquor dispensary. Fortunately for the drinking crowd, a local hero named Jessie Tuten filed a permit with the proper authorities in Columbia and planned to open for business as soon as his permit was approved. The county's first liquor dispensary was completed that summer and was located on South Carolina Highway 28 near the American Legion Hut in Hampton. Today, you can find a liquor store in almost every town in the county, but that didn't stamp out the thrill of making, selling and consuming illegal booze.

In February 1935, after national Prohibition was lifted, Roy Stone, the state's leading political prognosticator, conducted a statewide bootlegging survey. Hampton County's statistics were published in the *Guardian*. According to Stone's figures, the county still had seventy "inactive" bootleggers and sixty-one active operators selling as much as 1,879 gallons of whiskey per month.

However, R.O. Bowden, a well-known local banker and the county's "wet" leader, disputed those numbers and claimed there were at least three hundred bootleggers and distillers in the county putting out no less than six thousand gallons per month, adding that he knew one prominent distiller who was selling one thousand gallons a month alone. The wet banker made a point to add that he hoped the distilleries in the county kept running at full speed.

E.M. Peeples, the dry leader for the county, simply stated that he "knows nothing about bootlegging in his locality but that he is aware of the county being full of drunkards."

The taboo of "white lightning" moonshine and the daring appeal of the bootlegger smuggling his contraband across county lines just one step ahead of the law certainly enjoyed its place in local and even national history. But the allure of moonshine has transcended history and found its place in modern South Carolina as well.

Bootlegging still takes place in the Palmetto State, although on a much smaller scale. In October 2019, nearly ninety years after the repeal of Prohibition, Orangeburg County deputies busted a large moonshine operation near Holly Hill, a place that had been the target of several busts in recent years. Police seized an estimated $6,000 worth of illegal liquor and used axes and shotguns to destroy more than a dozen barrels that were actively fermenting moonshine.

Moonshine has now legally found a place on liquor store shelves, in bars and in the South Carolina tourism scene. In 2009, state laws were revised to allow micro-distilleries, and many businesses, such as Palmetto Moonshine, pay homage to our bootlegging history by selling legal moonshine using tried-and-true methods learned from former liquor lawbreakers. Today, moonshine can be found in many flavors in almost every liquor store in the state.

Does the hooch taste the same as it did back then? Or is it the thrill of the taboo, the appeal of indulging in the forbidden, that moonshine drinkers savor the most?

Let's have a snort and discuss it over a stiff drink, shall we?

RIPPED FROM THE HEADLINES

Author's note: As a journalist, I want the reader to experience the feel and flavor of reading history as it was written in the headlines of the day, just as if one were picking up the Thursday paper back in 1939, for example. I have included excerpts from several of my favorite news stories from local newspaper archives in this and the following chapters. Unless otherwise indicated, all news articles are from the *Hampton County Guardian*. The only edits made are to remove potentially offensive words like *Negro* or *colored* unless those words appear in a headline, are relevant to the story or are instrumental in illustrating the racist attitude of that era.

Hampton County Herald
March 22, 1917
Prohibition Rally to Be Held in Hampton
The Hon. Fred G. Bale of Ohio will speak at the Hampton Baptist Church next Sunday morning at 11:15. Mr. Bale represents the Anti-Saloon League of America and will speak on the great Prohibition Movement now being agitated in all parts of our country.

Hampton County Herald
January 11, 1918
[Author's note: I have heard more than one reference to "Suecat" or "Sue Cat" from family elders during my youth. Sue Cat was commonly made around Thanksgiving when the local sugarcane crop was ready for grinding into syrup. My family elders said that if you drank Sue Cat on Christmas Eve you wouldn't wake up until New Years. Must have been some powerful stuff.]
One Brother Kills Another
Men Drank "Suecat" or Cane Skimmings
Mallie and Earl Garner, brothers living near Mt. Carmel Church at Nixville, S.C., tried to celebrate the holidays by getting drunk on cane skimmings. A quarrel soon followed in which Earl drew a pistol. Mallie says he closed with his brother, took the gun away and shot him, but did not know he had killed him until the next morning when his father sent for him and told him of his crime. He has several scars and cuts from the fight.

Mallie Garner gave up and is in the Hampton jail awaiting trial.

This is the only crime for Hampton County during the holidays and was caused by this miserable drink made from cane juice.

Hampton County Guardian
June 18, 1919
Many Thirsty Citizens Here Kick on Blue Sunday Law
Hampton lived through last Sunday despite the fact that many of her thirsty citizens declared it was impossible to exist for one day without the aid of cool drinks, cigars, cigarettes, etc....A number of the citizens declared they would petition the city fathers to amend the law so that they could at least buy a Sunday paper.

October 26, 1921

Fairfax Policeman Shot by Alleged Bootleggers

On last Friday morning Chief of Police Harter of the town of Fairfax was shot and seriously wounded by a man who it is alleged was transporting contraband liquor. The suspect arrived on the Seaboard train early in the morning and was suspected from his actions by Chief Harter, who arrested him, and on the way to the lock-up, while discussing the matter of the arrest, the suspect shot Harter, the bullet striking the policeman in the head and inflicting a very painful if not serious wound. The wounded policeman was taken to Columbia to the Baptist Hospital where he lies in a rather critical condition.

The suitcase carried by the suspect was left on the scene, although the man has, to all appearances, made good his escape. The suitcase bore the name of D.C. Davis and contained two bottles of whisky. His coat, which was also left in the struggle, contained another bottle of liquor.

Every means is being used by the county officers to apprehend and bring the bootlegger to prison, but to all appearances he has left the county for good.

August 15, 1923

Morris Smalls Is Shot in Back
Killed While Plowing in Field. Motive Thought to Be Revenge.

The culmination of what is believed to be one of the best bits of detective work ever taking place in this county came on July 26, when Ishmael Fennell was arrested.

Morris Smalls was plowing his field in Yemasee about noon on July 6 when he was shot in the back from ambush with a load of buckshot. Suspicion was directed at once toward Fennell, who had a motive for revenge after Smalls led officers to a liquor still operated by Fennell, which resulted in the man's arrest.

In addition to a shotgun and shells found in Fennell's house that matched evidence at the crime scene, there was this incriminating, poorly written note Smalls received in the mail:

"Morris Smalls,

"I understand that you reported my nigrow [sic] for stilling whiskey and we do not want to hurt you and we will give you until June 18th to leave Hampton County. If not so abide by whatsoever may happening. First and last notice…"

There was no name signed.

Solicitor Randolph Murdaugh represented the state in this case.

August 19, 1925

Negro Said to Have Sold Poisoned Liquor

Joe Hicks was last week released from custody under $1,000 bond while awaiting returns from a sample of liquor which was sent off by Sheriff Thomas for examination to see if it contained poison.

Bob Fraser died on Aug. 8 and it is alleged that he met his death as a result of drinking a portion of a bottle of liquor which is said to have been sold by Hicks. The coroner's report states that Fraser met his death from effects of poison in the liquor he drank. Accordingly, Hicks was arrested, charged with selling Fraser the liquor which was supposed to have caused his death. Until the examination has been made it will not be known whether the liquor really contained poison or not. And then it will have to be proven that Hicks was the party that sold the liquor. So, in the meantime the alleged moonshine killer is enjoying his freedom under bond for appearance when wanted.

March 2, 1927

Blue Law Leaves Thirsty Citizens Sunday

Reports are current at the county seat that the only drink sold in this county on last "Blue" Sunday was moonshine liquor. Rumor has it that bootleggers did a whirlwind business as the result of the antiquated Sunday law. One story making the rounds is that when a thirsty man called on his favorite bootlegger for relief Sunday, he had no trouble obtaining corn whiskey, but when he asked for a bottle of ginger ale to use as a chaser the moonshiner declared he could not sell the ginger ale on Sunday because it was against the law.

While "Blue Sunday" was not very popular in the county, Hampton's new Intendant, D.B. Parker, approved of the law.

"The first Sunday that the law was enforced here added greatly to the attendance at Sunday Schools and churches," he said. "There were very few drunkards or loafers on the streets. Why? Because there were no places for them to hang around. Where there is a store or any place of business open on Sunday, there is where the drunkards and loafers are going to hang around. It is natural for a drunkard to want to be among others to see and be seen. If there is any congregating on Sunday, let it be in the churches."

May 9, 1956

Bootleg Suspect Dies in Auto Chase

In a wild chase ending as tragically as a Hollywood thriller, John Baggett of Colleton County died after crashing into a pine tree on old Salkehatchie Road between Early Branch and Yemassee about 11 p.m. Friday.

Officers said the car was heavily loaded with bootleg liquor and in pursuit of the man was Yemassee's police chief and a county constable, Early Youmans. Officers said they had received a tip that Baggett would be hauling liquor through the county and had spotted him in Yemassee. The moonshine runner had tried to run the police cars off the road several times before crashing himself, the lawmen added.

5

UNHOLY DEEDS

Throughout the years, the church has been an important facet of life in rural southern locations like Hampton County. People cleaned up good at least once a week, donning their "Sunday finest," for long sermons, heartfelt hymns and dinner on the grounds. The church was also a social gathering place, a place to make business connections, even a place to learn the latest gossip.

While it is almost impossible to know how many churches have come and gone in Hampton County over the years, modern publications of the *Hampton County Guardian* listed the most recent tallies at more than 110. With the county being 559 square miles in size, that is roughly 1 church for every 5 square miles.

So important was the local church in our Bible Belt, Lowcountry culture that, throughout the 1930s, the *Guardian* inserted a header across the top of its front pages almost every week that read "Our Churches and Schools Are Unexcelled!"

But throughout local history, some unholy deeds have occurred in even the holiest of places: the country church. Perhaps the most horribly wicked unholy deed takes us from the bloodstained pews of a country church in southern Hampton County all the way to the electric chair on death row in the state capital of Columbia.

The April 12, 1922, headline of the *Guardian* read: "Negro Is Slain While Praying: Estill Church Is Scene of Murder on Sunday Afternoon."

While kneeling in an attitude of prayer, taking the holy communion at the altar of a church at Estill, Thaddeus Fulton, reported to be a first cousin to the famous desperado, Richard Henry Austin, was shot and killed by another man, Jake Terry, at about four o'clock Sunday afternoon. Five of the six bullets fired from the pistol in the hands of Terry penetrated the body of Fulton, killing him instantly.

It seems that some old grudge existed between the parties and when Terry went to church, on finding his antagonist there, he rushed back to Estill, procured a 38 Special pistol and a box of bullets, and returned to the church. On entering the church, he found Fulton kneeling at the altar partaking of bread and wine in the community service. It is said that without hesitation he walked up to the victim, pulled his pistol, and fired six times. He reloaded his pistol and rushed back to Estill, where he endeavored to secure some money that was owed to him. He then hurriedly left Estill, taking to the woods.

As soon as the matter was reported to officers, a posse was formed, and Terry was surrounded in a swampy place near Estill. After an exchange of gunfire with officers, the murder suspect briefly evaded capture. After nearby towns were alerted, Terry was later apprehended in Fairfax after another exchange of gunfire in which the suspect was shot at least twice by police. On being taken into custody, he was sent to Roper Hospital in Charleston for lifesaving surgery before being incarcerated.

In what was called "a crime unparalleled in the history of Hampton County" by the *Guardian*, Terry was convicted of murder in the May 1922 term of court, during which time he appeared in the courtroom lying on a cot, still suffering from his officer-involved shooting wounds. During the trial, Terry claimed that before he opened fire, he saw a gun in Fulton's hand. In contrast to claims that the deceased victim had been praying and taking communion, Terry maintained that the collection plate was being passed at the time of the shooting.

The conviction was appealed by his attorneys, however, causing a stay of execution and a retrial in February 1923. Terry was sent back to the state pen, where it was reported he continued to suffer for months from his wounds and was mostly confined to the prison's infirmary. The condemned man's limbs were wrapped in "plaster of Paris," and he could not move.

That appeal was denied, but it was necessary to resentence Terry. During the retrial, Judge T.S. Sease showed no mercy and resentenced the convicted murderer to die in the electric chair at the state penitentiary on March 2,

1923. But shortly after the retrial, South Carolina governor Thomas G. McLeod granted a brief reprieve until March 16 so he could fully investigate the matter and learn all the facts before allowing Terry to be executed.

This further delay prompted an outcry from several citizens in the community, who entered a protest with the governor, calling attention to the fact that this brutal deed was committed in, of all places, a church. After considering the case, the governor decided not to intervene.

Terry was set to die on Friday, March 16. Oddly, the official witness to his execution for killing a man in a church on a Sunday was a man named Billy Sunday, a famous evangelist. In reporting Terry's death, the *State* paper wrote, "Pitying eyes witnessed the execution of the negro who was disabled by gunshot wounds and had to be carried from his cell in the death house to the electric chair," with Billy Sunday walking behind him, offering up a prayer.

After Terry was strapped to the chair and the death warrant was read, a prison superintendent asked if he had anything to say. Terry responded, "The Lord is my shepherd, I shall not want," and then proceeded to recite the Twenty-Third Psalm. He "continued to call on the Lord to have mercy on him until the switch sent the death dealing current through his body."

Officials reported that Terry made no mention of the murder, nor did he ask for forgiveness of his crime. It was also reported that the execution was witnessed by "the smallest number of persons ever known" at the state penitentiary and that Hampton County citizens were not represented. Terry had no friends or family there to comfort him or claim his body.

Terry's remains were later interred in the prison burying ground.

RIPPED FROM THE HEADLINES

June 27, 1923
Thieves Caught with the Goods
Stole Car While Owners in Church, Caught on Highway Near Aiken
What is believed to be one of the boldest auto thefts ever perpetrated in this part of the State was committed on last Sunday night during services at the Baptist Church in Varnville. The car belonging to Mr. P.B., driven by Mr. W. Patrick., was stolen from in front of the church, while Mr. P.B. was attending the services, and the loss not discovered until services were out.

Mr. P.B. immediately secured a car and set out in pursuit of the culprits. After a chase of over an hour, the pair were overhauled on the highway between Augusta and Aiken in possession of the stolen car.

The town of Varnville was considerably excited when the news had spread, the nerve of the robbers making a distinct impression on the populace.

The car was recovered intact, and the thieves were checked into the Hampton County Jail.

February 2, 1949

[Author's note: Sometimes the unholy can be converted into holy use; at least that was the case with one moonshine operation.]

Moonshine Still Makes Church Dome

Confiscated moonshine equipment (now consecrated) is the source of a halo for the bell tower of the beautiful new Hampton Methodist Church, now nearing completion, according to information received this week from Sheriff Alton M. Lightsey and Deputy H.C. Mixon, who donated the confiscated copper.

Sheriff Lightsey and Deputy Mixon gave the church copper confiscated when they raided some 10 illicit liquor stills in the county. The copper still was hammered out under the direction of Mr. Roberts, a member of the church, and has been used as a copper dome for the bell tower.

September 13, 1950

[Author's note: The readers should best decide for themselves who the unholy parties are in this historical scandal.]

Blue Law Jails Theater Owners

Hampton's Sunday movie squabble turned into open controversy over the weekend when the co-owners of the Palmetto Theater were arrested for showing movies on a Sunday.

The pair of prominent Hampton men, T.G. Stanley, mayor pro-tem of Hampton, and a businessman, and Dr. J.A. Hayne Jr., family physician, was arrested at the theater during the Sunday night show, "Wake Island," on a warrant served by Deputy Sheriff H.C. Mixson.

Mixson was the same officer credited with scores of moonshine arrests in that era. The warrant was sworn out by the Reverend Lewis E. McCormick, pastor of Hampton Baptist Church; the Reverend O.S. Ulmer, pastor of

The Palmetto Theater in Hampton, when it was a working movie theater in April 1970. *Courtesy of the* Hampton County Guardian *archives*.

Brunson Baptist Church; and the Reverend B.H. Covington, pastor of Hampton Methodist Church. The warrant was issued under an old South Carolina blue law that prohibited operation of moving-picture theaters on Sundays. Stanley and Dr. Hayne were charged with "unlawful operation of a motion picture theater, against the statutes in such cases provided against the peace and dignity of the state."

The two arrestees were transported from the theater to the jail by Deputy Mixson. Solicitor Randolph Murdaugh and the three ministers signed the warrant.

Hampton mayor J.L. Holland arrived at the jail shortly after the men were locked in and paid $100 bond each to release the men from the Hampton County jail. The case was set to go to trial before Magistrate Coy Thomas.

After their release, Stanley and Dr. Hayne made the following statement to the *Guardian*:

We consider it [closing movies on Sunday] *a discriminatory action and object on these grounds. The same South Carolina outdated Blue Laws banned the delivery of newspapers on Sunday, operation of trains, operation of service stations, swimming pools and drug stores. We have previously written letters to the ministers of the county saying we will cooperate fully if they will treat all businesses alike in this close-up campaign.*

Reportedly, the co-owners had been showing movies since the first of May because of popular demand, and the showings were well attended, despite opposition from the churches and a petition circulating around the county.

The committee of ministers declined to give the *Guardian* a statement after the arrests, but it was believed that their next target was going to be the Fairfax drive-in, located just inside Hampton County.

February 19, 1964

Judge Adds Church Going to Sentence

Judge Julius Ness caused "plenty of surprise" in Hampton County General Sessions Court. The terms of probation for two teenagers pleading guilty to housebreaking and grand larceny included mandatory Sunday School and church attendance—for five years.

The judge, who was known for this type of sentencing, also required full restitution, refraining from alcoholic beverages, and securing and keeping gainful employment for two to three years.

STICKY PALMS AND
THE FIVE-FINGER DISCOUNT

From hog rustlers to white-collar criminals, from petty thieves and dumb crooks to ingenious con artists, thievery fills the pages of history in Hampton County.

Sticky palms. The five-finger discount. Call it what you will, stealing is stealing, and it's among the most popular of sins on all seven continents. But here in the rural, agrarian South, thievery has taken some interesting forms over the years.

Hampton County history is filled with interesting reports of wicked people (or poor folks just trying to survive, depending on how you choose to look at it) stealing the fruits of the land. Here, stolen goods often included bales of cotton, farm animals, timber and crops like corn or watermelons—both by the melon and by the truckload. You know what they say, the forbidden fruit tastes sweeter.

The history of the Wild West is filled with tales of thieves "rustling" herds of cows under the light of the moon, but have you ever heard of a hog rustler? While not as romantic and manly as the western rustlers, who sat high on horseback, bearded faces masked by bandanas and shaded by ten-gallon cowboy hats, hog rustlers were quite common in the Lowcountry even if they didn't ride off into the sunset on horses. Consider the case of Sammy R., an energetic Brunson man who had himself quite a fine time on a chilly night in November 1959. Sheriff A.M. DeLoach reported to the *Guardian* that Sammy stole a 1950 Ford car from Rob Willie Brooker's "juke joint" in Brunson that Friday night, then stole a hog from his sister's house, then apparently threw the porker inside the car and went for a ride.

The report did not mention why the hog was stolen—was it for sale on the black market, for barbecue purposes or perhaps for companionship? —but Sammy and the pig must have had a mighty fine time, because in addition to grand larceny and hog rustling, Sammy was charged with driving under the influence. His porky pal was not charged.

Stolen hogs once played a role in an attempted railroad fraud case that ended in a fatal shootout. On May 5, 1916, the *Hampton County Herald* reported that an unscrupulous hog man placed some dead hogs on the Seaboard Air Line Railway track in Scotia, a small community in southern Hampton County, and was planning on filing a false claim that the train had killed his poor pigs. When the foreman of the railroad confronted the suspect, pistols were produced, and the hog man was fatally wounded in the ensuing shootout.

In the interest of full disclosure, I must confess to you that one of my distant and now departed relatives who was known to indulge in moonshine-related activities was also infamously known as the best (or worst, depending on how you look at it) hog rustler in the history of Hampton County.

To give you an idea of his kleptomaniac nature, according to family legend, Cousin S. was arrested once after a three-night stealing spree. The first night, he relieved a prominent Estill farmer of the burden of feeding a small herd of healthy hogs. The next night, he went back to the same farm and stole a few bushels of corn to feed the stolen hogs. What did him in, however, was when he decided to visit the scene of the crime on the third night to steal some fence and fence posts to keep his newfound herd from wandering off or going back home—and was promptly arrested.

Newspaper reports confirm the basics of his ample criminal record, but I haven't been able to confirm the stolen fence part. My family has been known to exaggerate a good story from time to time, but I would like to think it's true.

Cousin S. was also known to keep company with other questionable characters and was reportedly a friend of Randolph "Buster" Murdaugh Jr. Family stories claim that whenever Buster held a barbecue or "pig picking" for his law-enforcement and lawyer friends, Cousin S. was always there to cook the hogs for him.

It is unclear from these stories if our colorful cousin was simply the barbecue pitmaster or if he also provided the hogs. I've always wondered.

WHITE-COLLAR CRIMINALS

Until we rid the world of tax collectors and other public officials, there will exist the temptation to steal public money. Throughout its history, many of Hampton County's public officials have succumbed to that temptation.

In February 1921, former Hampton County treasurer W.A. Mason was indicted by the local grand jury with failure to turn over official moneys to his successor in office. The shortage was reported to be more than $17,000. At the same time, a former county supervisor, W.F. Harrison, was also charged with misappropriating funds.

While there were several murder cases on the docket, Solicitor Randolph Murdaugh Sr. said the Mason case was one of the most important to be tried, adding that the state intended to "push vigorously" against Mason.

Mason's case went to trial in June 1921. He was convicted, and Judge James E. Peurifoy, after refusing a motion for a new trial, sentenced the former public official to the maximum sentence for that crime: twelve months at hard labor on the county chain gang or in the state penitentiary and a fine of $1,000.

When corrupt government officials weren't stealing public money, they were trying to find new ways to pick taxpayers' pockets. Consider the following excerpt from the *Hampton County Guardian* after the county passed a controversial "dog tax" around 1921.

Dogs Ain't Dead Yet Here's the Money
Canine Survives Past Tax Limit and Owner Keeps His Word
In the *Guardian* of January 24, 1921, an article was published under the heading: "Not a Whole Dog on Place but Will Pay." This was a story of a county taxpayer who wrote to Treasurer Causey explaining that he had owned two dogs but one had died and the other had a broken leg and was not expected to live until time to close the tax books. The man went on to say, however, that if his dog did live, he would pay the taxes on him.

Treasurer Causey then received a follow-up letter from this man, short and to the point. The letter, exactly as written, is as follows:

> *Yemassee s c. feb 1ˢᵗ 23*
> *Mr re cossey dear sir please find enclose $125 to cover tax of one yellow three leg dog he is not Dead yet so I am sending the money request of me Hope the school will be better remain yours*
> *"Alex"*

While "the school" seemed to have left our letter writer lacking, the dog tax must have been a successful way for the government to fleece the citizens, because the article concluded with remarks from the treasurer about expanding the tax to include other animals.

While the pet tax had a happy ending for the taxman, this wasn't the case for many corrupt officials when their crimes were exposed. In June 1922, the crimes of a county commissioner may have caused him to take extraordinary measures.

June 14, 1922

County Commissioner Takes His Life at Early Branch

J.R. Taylor, a member of the board of county commissioners for Hampton County, committed suicide at his home in Early Branch early Wednesday morning, according to reports reaching Hampton today. Taylor had been present at the meeting of the board of county commissioners on Monday and was also in Hampton until about noon on Tuesday.

Rumors were afloat here Monday and Tuesday to the effect that certain irregularities existed in the payroll accounts under the supervision of Commissioner Taylor. It was also heard around the courthouse that an investigation was underway by the grand jury and that a subpoena had been issued by the foreman of the grand jury for the appearance of Taylor here this morning. It was also stated that Taylor was served with the subpoena Tuesday at his home.

Only meager details of the suicide are obtainable at this time. It appears that the deceased killed himself by firing a bullet from a revolver into his head about four o'clock Wednesday morning at his home near Early Branch.

June 21, 1922

County Officer Met Death by Accident Is Verdict of Jury

Joseph "J.R." Taylor, of Early Branch, former County Commissioner, came to his death by a self-inflicted pistol wound by accident at his home at four a.m. on Wednesday, according to a verdict returned by 12 citizens of Early Branch comprising the jury of inquest.

The full text of the verdict of the jury follows: We the jury impaneled to inquire into the death of Mr. T find that he came to his death by a self-inflicted pistol wound, and we believe it to have been an accident as he was returning up the steps into the house after going out to shoot a dog.

RIPPED FROM THE HEADLINES

Dumb Crooks

January 25, 1925
J.J. was arrested and lodged in the local jail Monday and is charged with the theft of several articles of clothing from the store of M.V. Stanley, his employer. Included in the loot were trousers, hats, shoes and an electrical flashlight. The man successfully got away with the merchandise, the police said, but he made the fatal mistake of wearing the stolen trousers to work.

Cunning Con Men

November 9, 1949
Gypsies Get $627 in Flim Flam Game
Sheriff A.M. Lightsey, his deputy H.C. Mixon and State Constable H.A. Stack spent a busy weekend searching for a pair of gypsies, thought to be in this vicinity, after they stole $627 from a woman, Rosa Lee Anderson, at McPhersonville last Friday.

The gypsies, thought to be a mother and daughter combination, pretended to be "healers" and promised to cure an afflicted member of Rosa Lee's family for a "reasonable fee."

The first donation of ten cents wasn't enough for the healers, so they asked for the family's savings to "hold" and wrapped the money in a road map, returning the map to them when they drove off. The family was instructed not to open the package for two hours, and upon opening, Rose Lee found she was left holding the bag, empty.

Hampton County Democrat
February 17, 1950
Guardian Contest Agent Arrested on Charge of Grand Larceny
No one was exempt from the long arm of the law, not even employees and representatives of the Hampton County Guardian.

On February 17, 1950, a rival newspaper, the Hampton County Democrat, quite possibly took great delight in announcing to its readers that William Nimmo, a subscription contest editor for the Guardian and the Allendale County Citizen, had been arrested on a warrant taken out *in Lake City, Florida, charging Nimmo with grand larceny of $1,300, according to Solicitor Randolph Murdaugh Jr.*

The warrant alleged that Nimmo stole $1,300 in connection with a newspaper subscription contest by telling people that if they put some of their own money into the contest, they could win the prize. After fleecing at least two people, Nimmo then left the county.

When asked for comment on the matter, Tom O'Conner, editor of the Guardian and the Citizen, simply said, "I have reason to believe certain disgruntled persons are trying to disrupt our contest," but he would not elaborate on who he was referring to.

November 6, 1957

Four Men Accused of Hog Rustling

This is the tale of five fat pigs who stayed home but got to market anyway.

Four men are being held in the Hampton County jail and charged with hog rustling, according to Sheriff A.M. DeLoach, whose office completed this case Monday.

They are charged with theft of more than $200 worth of hogs from the farm of Hampton County Auditor Jesse Thomas. The thieves "boldly hauled off five hogs in the daytime, killing at least or two of them right in the field."

"WILD EAST" OUTLAWS

Many of us grew up enjoying movies and black-and-white TV shows depicting the Wild West, a dusty historical landscape inhabited by outlaw gunslingers, warring Native American tribes and sassy saloon girls. Please allow me to introduce you to what I call the "Wild East."

In many ways, Hampton County of the late 1800s and early 1900s strongly resembled the old American West that captured the imagination of Hollywood and the paperback book industry. Livestock roamed the dirt streets, cattle and hog rustlers lurked about the countryside and there were enough gunfights and train or bank robberies to keep sheriffs busy and local newspaper editors hopping with their primitive printing presses. In addition, "whisky artists" made runs here and there, and from time to time the silence of the town's streets and the quiet countryside were penetrated by sounds of gunfire as bootleggers shot it out with the law while trying to make a getaway.

While the West had the OK Corral, Hampton had its "Horses and Asses" farm. While western bandits robbed stagecoaches crossing the dusty plains, Lowcountry locals robbed Yankees passing through on their way to sunny Florida—sometimes at gunpoint, but usually at roadside gambling houses. While outlaws were hanged from cottonwood trees west of the Mississippi, here, suspects were lynched in front of the county courthouse or right inside the county jail, often without the courtesy of a trial. Hampton County even had its version of saloon girls, or prostitutes. The county was populated with "road houses" and "tourist camps" so notorious that in February 1939, Circuit Court Judge M.M. Mann declared them "worse than the red light districts of the olden times."

While the citizens of the West had to face wolves and grizzly bears, here in the South Carolina Lowcountry, we had massive alligators and mammoth wild hogs to contend with. The giant porkers ranged in and out of the Salkehatchie and Coosawhatchie swamps, destroying farmland and sometimes even the occasional hapless hunter and his dogs. In September 1941, Tommie Jackson, an elderly Yemassee hunter, killed a mammoth hog weighing four hundred pounds with five tusks measuring five inches and bottom tusks of over three inches. Since then, much larger boars have been harvested in Hampton County. But wild hogs weren't the only problem. Once, as a Cummings farmer parked his truck on Lee Avenue to do some business, a market-sized farm hog escaped and was enjoying an afternoon "on the town." It took several merchants and volunteers to round up the stray hog.

Amid all this wildness, people managed to raise families, educate their children and still make it to church on Sunday. But some of them had a lot to pray about.

BLOODY KNUCKLE BRAWLS

While gunslinging rivals of Dodge City and Tombstone often challenged one another to pistol duels at high noon, at least according to the movies, sometimes, Hampton County countryside folks would come to town to settle their disputes on Main Street, under the landmark town clock or at the town's main fountain near Lee Avenue, as was the case of a February 1914 brawl that made the front page of the *Guardian*.

Kelvin Shuman and Horace Long were both from "the country," as the *Guardian* described it, and were relatives by marriage. But there was bad blood between them.

> *First Monday in Hampton was enlivened by one fight which was a most bitter one, one of the contestants being badly used up. The affray occurred right on the main street and caused a lot of excitement while it lasted....*
>
> *Long and Shuman locked horns near the fountain on Lee Avenue. They went at it hammer and tongs and Shuman was the under man. The fight lasted several minutes, Shuman being badly used up. His face was badly*

beaten and there were several bad cuts about his head. He was given medical attention and was taken home in the evening. Long was slightly hurt about the face and hands.

For a time, serious trouble was threatened, but cooler heads allowed the direct participants in the fight to have it out and no one but the two were allowed to interfere.

Gunfights and Timber Towns

Just as the Wild West had mining towns, Hampton County had timber towns. These timber and lumber villages were cities unto themselves, full of roughneck workers and often rougher foremen. In these places, the owners printed their own "scrip" money for employees to spend in the company-owned stores.

There were often disputes, such as the February 1914 gunfight at the Lightsey Mill between a member of the prominent Lightsey family and one of their employees.

"J.C. Lightsey, Jr., a well-known young man, is lucky that he escaped Monday with his life," wrote the *Guardian*. "He was fired at point blank by

The Bonneau Sawmill was one of several operating in Hampton County in the late 1800s and early 1900s. *Courtesy of the* Hampton County Guardian *archives.*

The Lightsey Brothers Sawmill in Miley, after a boiler explosion closed operations for nearly a year, around 1934. *Courtesy of the* Hampton County Guardian *archives.*

Wilber Owens, an employee of the Lightsey Mill, above town, and had Owens's aim been good, 'C' might have suffered serious hurts."

Lightsey had opened the lumber mill commissary about dinnertime, and when the men employed around the place came in for trade, Owens was among them. He wanted the men to stop work and shut J.C. Lightsey's mill down and was "called to account" by the younger Lightsey, who ordered Owens out of the commissary.

Everything appeared to be settled, but Owens returned with a shotgun, took aim and pulled the trigger. The aim appeared to have been bad or the distance too great for serious damage. One of the shots entered young Lightsey's cheek; others hit him on the chest and legs.

Fortunately for "C" Lightsey, several loyal employees rushed Owens and relieved him of his shotgun just as he was reloading, granting Lightsey a "miraculous escape" from death or serious injury.

"Ford Fever" versus Horseback

If you walked the streets of the local towns, you might find a bank, a smelly livestock stable and a general store on the same block. During the Wild East era, it was almost impossible to walk the streets of our fair towns without shooing hogs, cows, horses or other livestock out of one's path, or dodging out of their way, even on Lee Avenue, in the shadow of the county courthouse. In 1915 and again in 1926, the town of Hampton passed laws prohibiting livestock from running loose in the town. That same year, a law was passed setting the speed limit for those newfangled "autos" at twenty miles per hour (punishable by a fine of $100 or thirty days on the county chain gang).

By 1920, the town had passed an ordinance prohibiting anyone under the age of twelve from driving a car in town limits. By October 1924, "Ford Fever," as the *Guardian* called it, had overtaken many residents, causing wrecks between autos, between autos and pedestrians and between autos and horses or buggies. Quite a few riders and their horses were killed in those early collisions between the old modes of transportation and newfangled technology.

Drive-by shootouts also became a new problem for the Wild East folks. In response, there was an outcry for a rural police force to address the crossroads gunfights on Saturday nights and drunkards who "puncture the air with bullets" while driving home at midnight. Eventually, the local undertaker invested in an automobile, or "horseless hearse," as it was called then.

Safecrackers and Train Robbers

Like the rivers of the Lowcountry, train tracks bisect the Hampton County landscape. A rail line runs from Brunson at the northern end of the county south to Yemassee, and another runs from Fairfax south to Garnett, as freight, mail and passengers are transported around South Carolina and Georgia. These trains were popular with criminals, who robbed them or used them for getaways after committing other robberies.

In addition to trains, other popular targets for robbers were post offices. Criminals known as "fences" in Charleston and elsewhere would pay eight to ten cents on the dollar for stolen stamps, and they also bought bonds and other valuables. In 1919 alone, there was a train robbery in June and a post office robbery in November. Even the "mom-and-pop" general stores that dotted the countryside were often hit. In 1933, safecrackers blew the door off a safe in a Cummings general store—along with all the store's windows and several display cases. Nothing was sacred: churches were often robbed, and in January 1932, a Coca-Cola truck of the Hampton Bottling Works was held up and robbed at gunpoint beyond Whippy Swamp, near Miley. Many would agree that it takes a low-down varmint to rob the Coca-Cola man.

While most of the common thieves and burglars were local, the more sophisticated hold-up men and safecrackers were generally from out of town and often part of larger operations. In September 1941, Sheriff Alton M. Lightsey questioned five men who were part of a new gang that sprang up in the county, robbing safes in the Rivers' store in Hampton and the Shuman store in Cummings over the summer. After interrogating the suspects, the sheriff learned that the gang was a subsidiary of Al Capone's once famous Chicago gang and that the organized criminals were operating throughout the Southeast.

Notorious Bank Robber "West Philadelphia Johnnie"

One big-time gangster operating in Hampton County was known as "West Philadelphia Johnnie" and was so notorious that he made the pages of New York newspapers.

In 1914, the *New York World* printed as a serial the confessions of John F. McCarthy, known in the realm of crooks as "West Philadelphia Johnnie," and Edward Henry Smith, and one of those confessions was reprinted in the *Guardian* in October of that year. These confessions, whether completely true or not, gave an insight into many of their crimes, including the robbery of the Bank of Brunson in northern Hampton County, which occurred on the night of November 3, 1908.

The central character in this robbery is the poor, comic victim: the lazy, fat night watchman who was found asleep in a wagon. The gangsters woke him up and made him go to a blacksmith shop with them to get a few materials they needed, then tied him up at the train depot. Billy, one of the robbers, force-fed him apples to calm him and allay his fears.

Billy remained at the train station with his prisoner while another robber stood guard at the bank. The others jimmied a window open, got into the bank and began working on the safe.

The first explosion on the vault was light and caused no commotion, but the night watchman began groaning, both out of fear and possibly because he was getting full of apples. The safecrackers got the vault door open with a couple more "shots" of explosives and started on the "kiester" (the inside of the vault). The shot on that made a "whale" of a noise that was sure to alarm everyone in town, the mobster recalled.

"Mister," the old watchman said to Billy, "Throw me under dis platform. There's going to be some shootin' and I don't wanna get hit."

Billy fed him more apples. At every apple, and every subsequent explosion, he'd groan and beg again to be put out of harm's way.

The kiester in this bank was a good one and slow to yield, West Philadelphia Johnnie recalled, so they risked a heavy charge and blew the thing wide open. The sound of the explosion was extraordinarily loud.

The old night watchman grunted so hard that he spit out a mouthful of apple.

In the vault the robbers found silver, gold and paper money amounting to about $800. The crooks then placed a chair in the broken vault, tied

The Loan and Exchange Bank in Hampton. *Courtesy of the* Hampton County Guardian *archives*.

the night watchman to it and gagged him, leaving him ten or twelve silver dollars for his trouble.

The four bandits carried the heavy bags of coins to a nearby shanty, broke into that and stole a handcar. They then made their way several miles down the tracks to the junction of the Seaboard Air Line. They hid the money in the woods and rested a short distance away. Around 11:00 p.m. that night, they recovered the money and stowed away on a coal train.

"Next came one of the unforeseen and unforeseeable things in robbing," recalled McCarthy. "Our freight train stopped in Brunson and shot our car into a side track smack in front of the bank we had robbed the night before. We waited until 1 o'clock and snuck out of the car. Then we began to hike in earnest. Luckily, near morning we got another train and succeeded in making our way to Charleston in two days."

Meanwhile, bankers and police found the poor tightly bound night watchman inside the blown vault, sick from the nitrogen fumes around him and covered with silver dollars and bits and pieces of apple.

BANKER BOWDEN

Just as some bank robbers became infamous up and down the East Coast, one local banker made a unique name for himself, both in Hampton County and nationally. While he wasn't an outlaw, Ralph Olen Bowden, commonly known as "Banker Bowden" or "Old Man Bowden" by locals, was known as a colorful character who played by his own rules and made national news for becoming close friends with a notorious but reformed bank heister.

In 1907, Bowden opened the Loan and Exchange Bank, which he co-owned with William Mauldin, on Hampton's main street. Bowden later purchased and erected Hampton's landmark clock on Lee Avenue.

Bowden wasn't the only banker in town, but he was without a doubt the most eccentric, and he didn't give a damn who liked it or not. He ran a simple but practical business: two bare electric light bulbs hung from the ceiling, there were only three adding machines and all accounts were posted by hand. A Confederate flag was draped over the front façade of his bank and others were flown out front until 1955, when he sold the business and the building to the Laffitte family, which now operates Palmetto State Bank.

Bowden was known for granting customers unusual loans and often asking for even more unusual collateral. A supporter of the "wet," or pro-alcohol movement, Bowden would loan money for such suspicious items as copper

AND ONCE AGAIN—The Flag of the Confedracy, flying before the Loan and Exchange Bank of Hampton, on Melon Day, signifies that old tradition is still revered in the Lowcountry.

A news clipping from the *Hampton County Guardian* depicting the Confederate flags flying at the Loan and Exchange Bank. *Courtesy of the* Hampton County Guardian *archives*.

tubing, barrels and other items often associated with the construction of a moonshine liquor still. He knew a smart, thriving business plan when he saw one. He would even loan money to farmers for livestock such as mules. After one such case, when questioned by an external bank examiner, Bowden had the mule brought in and showed him that because it had good teeth and a shiny, healthy coat it was a safe investment.

According to his family, Banker Bowden once even loaned money with people as collateral. In "Salkehatchie Stew" interviews conducted by the author for a University of South Carolina–Salkehatchie history project, his descendants recalled the exchange between a new, young doctor, fresh out of med school, who moved to town with nothing but his hat in his hand, to ask for a loan. When Bowden asked what the doctor had for collateral, he said he had nothing at the moment but his wife and children. So Old Man Bowden got their names and ages and put them down as collateral for the loan.

However, the old-fashioned banker was hesitant to make loans on modern items like automobiles. The following paraphrased story was shared with the author during a 2010 "Salkehatchie Stew" interview with Dawn Bowden Gibson, the banker's great-granddaughter, and recalls a conversation between a local customer, Eddie Ginn, and Bowden.

Ginn, then a young man excited about the prospect of purchasing a Ford Model A, drove the car right up to the front door of the bank to ask the Hampton banker for a loan to cover it.

While looking the car over, Bowden said, "You know, this looks nice, but I just don't know that I'm comfortable loaning you the money on this contraption."

"What do you mean, Mr. Bowden," young Eddie said, dumbfounded. "Sir, this is the finest, most innovative, newest thing they have come out with the whole industry of cars!"

"Well, I hate to tell you, but I'd almost rather loan you money on a mule than on this car, because this thing can break down and it will be no good to me."

"Well, Mr. Bowden, I understand that, and I hear where you're coming from," said an exasperated Eddie, "but I could also pick up a gun, and shoot that damn mule, and then you can't use the mule, either!"

The old banker frowned for a moment, then smiled and relented. "Come on in the bank, Sonny. Let's sit down and talk about this loan."

Hampton banker R.O. Bowden in front of the clock on Lee Avenue, 1950s. *Courtesy of the* Hampton County Guardian *archives.*

While he didn't know much about Fords, the banker knew mules. As a side business, he owned a livestock stable called Horses and Asses, located where Rigdon's Fried Chicken is today. (Rigdon's is a local landmark of sorts today. Located beside the railroad track, its owners claim their chicken is good enough to stop a train.) A youngster named Dan Black kept things going at Horses and Asses while Bowden ran the bank.

Horses and Asses also proved beneficial to Bowden when the federal bank regulators came to town to conduct an audit. The old banker often kept more money than he was supposed to in the bank, so when he got word that the feds were coming for inspection, he would wrap the excess cash in an old feed sack, then summon the faithful

Dan Black to bury it in a corner of the livestock stable, beneath the straw and manure.

Bowden was known for giving out strange loans with strange collateral while ignoring a few banking regulations here and there, but it paid off: His was reportedly the only bank that survived during the Great Depression in Hampton.

BANKER, BANK ROBBER BECOME UNLIKELY FRIENDS

While his antics made him widely known throughout the county, an unlikely friendship with a notorious former bank robber would send Bowden to New York City to appear on NBC's radio and TV programs.

In October 1950, Bowden made national headlines when he entertained one of the country's most infamous bank robbers at his Savannah River fish camp, Pink Ridge Hill: James "Big Jim" Morton of Cleveland, Ohio.

This strange banker–bank robber friendship developed after Bowden read the *Saturday Evening Post* series on Morton, "I was the King of Thieves," and decided it would be interesting to meet such a criminal "artist." Bowden then wrote a lengthy letter to Morton and, after a brief exchange of correspondence, invited Big Jim to visit him.

"Ralph is the first banker, and probably will be the last, to invite me to his home," Morton told the press. "Though I did notice the invitation was to his Savannah River place and not to his home in Hampton near the bank."

In response, Bowden said, "I imagine I must be the only banker in the world who would entertain a yeggman [a burglar or safecracker]. Jim, to me, looks like a Christian gentleman and has every earmark of a statesman, fine manners and he is handsome, too. I consider him a literary artist as well as a torch artist."

While enjoying a fine dinner at the fish camp, the inquisitive banker had a slew of questions for the reformed robber.

> *"What was the biggest haul you ever made?" he asked.*
> *"$184,000, from safety deposit boxes in an Indiana bank."*
> *"Do you think a robber would ever try a night depository like the one I had installed at my bank some time ago?"*
> *"No experienced robber would break it because he'd know in a town like Hampton it wouldn't be enough to make it worth the effort."*

Banker R.O. Bowden (*left*) and notorious former bank robber James "Big Jim" Morton examining a bank safe in October 1950. *Courtesy of the* Hampton County Guardian *archives.*

When asked by a reporter if he had ever robbed one of Bowden's banks, Big Jim replied, "No, I haven't robbed The Loan and Exchange Bank— that is, not yet."

Looking at a photo taken of the two in front of the safe at Bowden's bank, it would be difficult to guess at first glance who the professional banking officer was and who the ex-criminal was. Morton was clean cut and well attired, while Bowden appeared wild-haired and plainly dressed.

Bowden and Morton later traveled to New York, where they made a hit on the *We the People* nationwide Thursday night radio broadcast and its Friday night television show.

"Radios in this section were tuned in to NBC for the Thursday night broadcast and many persons saw the show," reported the *Guardian*. "Most persons commenting who heard the show said it was a real thrill to hear, "We take you to Hampton, South Carolina...."

RIPPED FROM THE HEADLINES

December 2, 1925

Brunson Man Shoots Player

Carnival Man Meets Death in Scuffle over Pistol in Brunson Café Last Week

A "friendly" scuffle over a pistol in the café of H.G. Downing last week resulted in the death of Slim Love, one of the players in the Knickerbocker Shows, then playing at the Hampton County Fair in Brunson.

Mr. LT, of the Buick Agency at Brunson, and Mr. A.G., parachute jumper for the Knickerbocker Shows, were scuffling for the possession of a 45 Colt automatic, when the tragedy took place. The gun went off unexpectedly, shooting Love through the abdomen. He was at once rushed to the hospital, but there was no possibility of saving his life. In the race with death, death won, the injured man breathing his last before he reached the hospital.

The shooting was declared accidental, and neither LT or AG, it is understood, will be held on a charge of murder or manslaughter. It is possible that a minor charge will be brought against one or both of the scufflers, but this is problematic at the present writing.

March 13, 1929

Loan & Exchange Robbed

Bandits Blow Safe, Take over $9,000

The Loan and Exchange Bank at Hampton has been a popular place since the robbery that took place last Friday morning, when $9,600 in real money and one to two thousand in coupon bonds were taken. Curious folks have journeyed from all over this section to have a look at the vault and the safe, which R.O. Bowden, general cashier, has been so kind to place on exhibit in the lobby of the bank so that all may see.

The robbers brought water in tubs and buckets into the bank and used it immediately after they had burned a hole with a blow torch into the vault and into the safe. The hole in the vault was big enough for a man to get his hand through. The water in the safe was still boiling hot when Mr. Bowden got to the bank after the robbery, and he knows they must have had a time fishing the money out of the hot water.

The alarm was given by C.S. Blocker, who was occupying a cot in the little ice house just across the street from the bank, and being aroused by the purring of an automobile, watched a man who was on guard outside of the bank until the man, sighting him, fired his gun. Mr. Blocker returned the fire and the men, four in all, leaped into a large car parked in back of the bank.

No arrests have been made.

MYSTERIOUS DISEASES AND DEATHS

The influenza germ is so small that it cannot be seen without a microscope, and yet people have been trying to shut it out by the coarse meshes of flu masks.
—Hampton County Guardian *of February 1919, revealing that during the deadly 1918 flu pandemic people were skeptical of wearing masks, much like during the recent COVID-19 pandemic.*

*D*isease and death were regular visitors to our ancestors in Hampton County, and the door was always open.

For Hampton, like other rural areas around the South, the previous centuries were an era of low-tech medicine, poor nutrition and sanitation and religion-fueled superstition. It was an age of parasite infections, lockjaw and rabid dogs roaming the dirt streets. The newspapers of that day contained ads for all sorts of miracle cures for just about any ailment. There were tonics, pills and powders for the relief of high blood pressure; energy for women; stomach worms for livestock; 666 for headaches, colds and fever; Swamp Root for weak kidneys; syrup of figs for a child's bowels—all right alongside advertisements for fortune tellers and miraculous healers.

Serious illness even played a role in the first Hampton County Watermelon Festival. Now a South Carolina tradition and billed as the oldest continual festival in the state, the first watermelon festival was held in July 1939 and featured queens and out-of-town dignitaries (many of whom flew in by plane), a golf tournament, a swimming meet and dancing to music by the City of Savannah Police Band.

The event also featured some questionable culinary practices and uninvited food-borne guests. Here is an excerpt from a July 12, 1939, *Guardian* article:

Several Stricken Ill

At least 30 persons were stricken ill Tuesday after having eaten chicken pilau at Hampton County's first watermelon festival. Two city aldermen and more than a dozen members of the Savannah police band became violently ill. Several people from Walterboro, including Rep. Jesse D. Padgett, were stricken. Six or eight from Hampton, one from Ridgeland, a Cummings resident, six from Furman and five from Estill were poisoned. Rep. Padgett was given a blood transfusion at the hospital in Waterboro Tuesday night. Two men from Walterboro flew to Hampton but returned home in an ambulance.

These were just some the common ailments of the era. There were far more deadly diseases out there waiting to claim lives.

Few diseases frightened people more in those days of less advanced medicine than did polio, also called infantile paralysis or the "Maiming Death." This scourge usually struck in the warm summer months, sweeping through towns like an epidemic every few years, causing temporary or permanent paralysis and even death. Though most people recovered quickly, some victims remained disabled for life.

Polio, or poliomyelitis, would make local headlines throughout the 1950s and into the 1960s. Headlines like "Fourth Case of Polio Reported in Area" were common, as were stories of national fundraising campaigns and polio vaccine clinics. There were also the occasional heartbreaking but inspiring stories of survivors, such as the disabled child who was fighting to walk but wanted to play football like his friends.

Some diseases, mysterious at the time, were deadly enough to drive men to madness—and sometimes even murder—but could have been avoided and easily treated.

DRIVEN TO MADNESS AND MURDER BY STARVATION

A March 4, 1914, article in the *Guardian* revealed a shocking but surprisingly curable disease that many people of that era, usually in poor or rural populations, suffered from: pellagra. The term *pellagra*, from *pelle agra*, Italian for "rough skin," is a nutritional deficiency disease caused by a lack of vitamin

B3 (niacin) in the diet. Its symptoms have historically been characterized by the 4 Ds: dermatitis, diarrhea and dementia leading to death. Symptoms also include mouth sores and inflamed skin, with areas exposed to sunlight affected first. Over time, the victim's skin becomes darker and stiffer before it peels off or bleeds. Left untreated, most patients die.

The term *pellagra* was first used in Spain in 1735, but it was a global disease affecting people where the diet is primarily maize- or corn based. The disease was endemic in southern Europe for nearly two hundred years before it was recognized in the United States in the early twentieth century.

By the early 1900s, pellagra had become an epidemic throughout the poor, rural South, where many people lived on a diet of mostly meat, molasses and cornmeal, which does not contain the type of niacin our bodies can break down.

For centuries, pellagra was misunderstood, misdiagnosed and mistreated. Some doctors thought it was a skin disease; others thought it was caused by spoiled food or toxins in corn. Then scientists and physicians discovered that this ailment was diet based and could be easily treated. Sadly, because the mysterious disease caused dementia and extremely erratic behavior, many victims found themselves in mental hospitals or "insane asylums."

In March 1914, the *Guardian* reported that more than 900 people around the state later found to have suffered from pellagra had been committed in previous years to the South Carolina Lunatic Asylum, also known as "Bull Street" for the street where it was located. In 1913 alone, 165 South Carolinians died from this misunderstood malady—many while locked away in psychiatric hospitals.

Pellagra was reported in almost every county of the state. From 1907 to 1913, Spartanburg led the state with eighty-three cases, while Richland County had eighty-two. Due to its smaller population and the fact that rural isolation combined with fewer doctors often led to the underreporting of cases, Hampton reported only seven pellagra cases during that time. But even some of those proved deadly.

In May 1933, a local man, sick and down on his luck, went mad and nearly committed an unthinkable act of violence on his family. He had been out of work for some time and, driven sick with hunger and worry about how to get money to buy food and clothes for his family, hadn't slept in three nights.

One Sunday, the Hampton man, who had been suffering from pellagra and diabetes, suddenly warned his wife to hide all the weapons in the house before he hurt some of the family members. On Monday morning, at sunrise, the man again woke with an overwhelming urge to kill his family and himself, rose before any of his family, walked into the yard in the early morning hours and returned with an axe.

His wife was awakened by a loud noise that proved to be the axe striking something. Driven mad by pellagra and poverty, the man had aimed the axe at his sleeping four-year-old daughter, but it hit the wall instead, striking the child only a glancing blow. His wife jumped from her bed and snatched up the axe.

"What in the name of God is the matter?" she screamed at her raving husband. Fortunately, she was able to get control of him until police could come and haul him away to the county jail. There, his words shocked doctors and law enforcement. "The devil is never dead," the madman said. "You fellows can take me out of here and kill me now."

Pellagra was a widespread cause of death until the early twentieth century, but the disease is curable with a proper diet, niacin supplements and other basic healthcare. Better nutrition and the widespread addition of niacin to flour have led to the practical eradication of this economically driven disease in developed countries.

But death can take many forms other than maddening disease, and when that call came, one man was always there to respond.

HAMPTON'S FAMOUS UNDERTAKER

"He has been thrown in the midst of heart aches and grief and has seen the Grim Reaper on rampaging campaigns."

These words were used by *Guardian* editors to describe Eugene M. Peeples, Hampton's longtime undertaker who ran Peeples Funeral Home in the days of horse-drawn hearses. The business also doubled as the local ambulance service.

Peeples began his career just after the turn of the century and served as an undertaker until the early 1950s. By 1939, after his first thirty-two years of service, Peeples told the *Guardian* that he had already handled more than four thousand bodies. The job included "sleepless nights, bodies mangled beyond recognition and cries of grief-stricken people," yet Peeples was known for his compassion, sympathy and giving solace to grieving families.

Born in Varnville in 1871, Peeples began working in Hampton as a funeral director in 1905 and became the undertaker in 1906. Death was his business, and business often came in the way of disease; gunshot wounds;

Hampton undertaker Eugene Peeples in the early 1900s, the days of the horse-drawn hearse. *Courtesy of the* Hampton County Guardian *archives.*

stabbings; railroad, sawmill or farming accidents; and even horse-versus-automobile crashes. From time to time, he would be called to transport a body back home to Hampton from the state "lunatic asylum" or, more often, bring home an expired prisoner from the state penitentiary who had been electrocuted or died of old age.

During the influenza epidemic of 1918, he worked day and night, often holding several funerals a day. Peeples recalled to the *Guardian* that, after going for days without sleep, he was so exhausted after preparing a body that he lay down beside the corpse and slept for three hours.

Then there was the occasional hunting accident or river drowning, including the almost miraculous but horribly tragic case involving a body that that been in the river for five years but was found strangely intact.

Emmett Charles Johnson drowned at Morris Landing on the Combahee River near Yemassee on March 18, 1944, as he attempted to save his thirteen-year-old handicapped son, Pete Johnson, who went into the water after their fishing boat capsized in the swift current.

The boy's body was found after a three-day search. After a futile three-month search for the father's body, Governor Olin D. Johnston called in the U.S. Coast Guard and U.S. Navy deep-sea divers from nearby bases to join in the hunt. The swamp was searched, and the river was dragged for days.

In late July 1949, a group of Yemassee teenagers found Johnson's body near Morris Landing while they were fishing on a Saturday morning. His body, strangely preserved, was discovered just a few miles from where he drowned.

The family was able to identify Johnson by a belt, belt buckle and gold key ring, still in good condition with the body. Peeples told the *Guardian* that this was the most unusual case on record here.

Peeples was known locally as a gifted "plastic surgeon" of sorts and could transform a mutilated face into something normal and pleasant looking for the grieving families. In a pinch, when a "preacher man" wasn't available, the beloved undertaker would fill in and perform funerals and memorial services.

Being employed in such a grim and morbid line of work was not without its lighter moments. Peeples recalled how he once had to obtain the false teeth of a dead man for his funeral from a friend and found out the man's friend had been wearing them. Once, while dressing a corpse for burial service, Peeples noticed that he had forgotten to put socks on the cadaver, so he discreetly pulled off his own and gave them as a parting gift to the dead man.

RIPPED FROM THE HEADLINES

June 15, 1949
Doctor Finds Medicine Bad Medicine in Court
A woman, who gave her name as Madam Williams, of Orlando, Fla., was fined $50 by Magistrate Coy Thomas on Monday for practicing "root doctoring." The formal charge was for practicing medicine without a license.

The woman was arrested by Chief of Police Mack Sullivan and Deputy H.C. Mixon. She has been living and practicing near Fetchtig, the officers reported. It was also reported that her concoctions have made several "patients" quite ill.

Dr. W.L. Salter, Hampton physician, was called in to the proceedings by Magistrate Thomas to scientifically analyze the collection of herbs, roots, etc., which were seized as evidence in the case, and he was able to identify several of the herbs.

July 12, 1950

Grave Election Matters Here Reported Nationally

As in the past Hampton precinct stepped into coffin boxes to mark their ballots and the fact drew nationwide attention when The Associated Press passed the tale along the wire. Despite the funeral atmosphere, said the AP dispatch, and the grave covering that held rain off voters outside the courthouse, the voters gave indications of being alive.

9
WICKEDNESS AT THE OLD JAIL

*I*f historic Hampton County had an epicenter of wickedness, it was the old Hampton County Jail.

The jail was a wicked hotbed of death, disease, discrimination and unlawful detainment. Wicked men and women were sent there, along with a few innocents, and wicked things were done to them. Men were lawfully hanged and unlawfully lynched there, and one county inmate even froze to death while locked away in a cage.

The original Hampton County Jail was commissioned by the South Carolina General Assembly in 1878 in tandem with the newly created Hampton County Courthouse and constructed in 1879–80. The upstairs portion of the jail was designed to house prisoners, while the jailer and his family and staff lived downstairs. Later, cells were added downstairs to house white females and other "special" prisoners.

This jail was meant to serve as a holding facility while county inmates awaited trial. Following conviction, prisoners were usually sent to state prisons or, in many cases, to their death sentences. But many who were confined in the jail found themselves in for more than just a temporary stay.

And many inmates didn't make it to see their day in court. The pages of the *Hampton County Guardian* are littered with stories of jailbreak lynchings, in which angry mobs stormed the facility—or were allowed to walk right in—to take out Black inmates for vigilante justice, which often included everything from whippings to shootings and hangings.

The old Hampton County Jail before it was taken out of public use. *Courtesy of the* Hampton County Guardian *archives*.

But vigilantes weren't the only executioners. According to Hampton County Historical Society and South Carolina Humanities Council records, during the early years of the jail's existence, one particularly harsh sheriff hanged an inmate from an iron bar inside the jail.

The prisoners had more to fear than early execution. The upstairs inmates were housed in iron cages about seven feet high with heavy iron doors that featured a triple lockdown system. For most of the jail's history, there was no waste plumbing, no lights, no running water, no heat in the winter, no fans and almost no air ventilation in the summer. Heavy blinds covered the barred windows so that meek and mild citizens wouldn't be exposed to the sight of the caged "convicts." In May 1919, the State Board of Charities and Corrections recommended some form of heat be installed after a jailer reported that a prisoner had frozen to death inside his cell the previous winter, "which is a shameful thing for a civilized community to allow," reported the *Guardian*.

The inmates used buckets for toilets, ate poor-quality food from tin plates (fresh meat and bread were limited) and slept on hard beds in the same clothes they were arrested in (the jail didn't provide uniforms until more modern times), unless family members brought them a change of clothing. Inmates slept on "pallets" made of blankets until sometime in 1917, when iron cots were added.

Most of the inmate space, a six-cell cage, housed the Black male prisoners. Adults and juveniles were housed together, but males and females were usually segregated. White and Black inmates were housed separately at almost all times. White prisoners were fed three times a day; Black inmates were fed only twice daily.

Medical care and hygiene were minimal, and inmates were not even vaccinated for diseases such as typhoid and smallpox, according to a May 1916 report in the *Guardian*. Inmates with communicable diseases were housed in the same cramped cells as uninfected inmates, sharing bedding, latrine buckets and eating utensils with healthy prisoners. The prisoners never bathed and often had to be deloused, bedding was usually washed and boiled only several times a year and the floors were cleaned just two or three times a year.

Whipping was used as punishment for errant inmates, and trustworthy inmates were allowed to cut wood for exercise in the jail yard or work in the jail kitchen.

THE HC "CHAIN GANG"

Some inmates were sentenced to hard labor year-round, and these chain gang prisoners were often kept in primitive camps around the county near where they were put to work, clearing forests for roads, digging ditches and working on farms. Conditions at these camps were just as horrid as inside the cramped jail.

In October 1917, the State Board of Charities and Corrections reported that inmates regularly washed in the same tub of water and were often whipped with a strap, both by the chain gang foreman and by trusted convicts acting under orders of the guards.

In May 1919, the Hampton County chain gang was rated below average by the State Board of Charities, and in July 1920, a report by Dr. G. Croft Williams, secretary of the State Board of Public Welfare, listed the Hampton County chain gang as one of the most unsatisfactory in the state. The report stated:

> *Sanitation at the Hampton County chain gang* [camp] *is far from what it should be. At the time of the visit the refuse pit was in a fearsome condition, both flies and stench being very much in evidence. The soil bucket for the cage was almost as great a menace to the health of the camp. The bedding was badly in need of washing. A prisoner suspected of having tuberculosis*

was being properly isolated during the day but was sleeping at night in the cage with the other men.

In January 1941, County Supervisor C. Murray Tuten ruled that county convicts could no longer be kept in camps but had to be placed in houses in a stockade located in a central part of the county.

JAIL REFORMS

According to state records, the conditions of the Hampton County Jail were most "deplorable" from 1914 to 1919. In 1919, the South Carolina State Board of Charities and Corrections rated this county jail as "one of the worse jails in the state."

The elected sheriffs during that shameful time in county history included Judson H. Lightsey (served 1902–13), Benjamin S. Williams (1913–14) and John Herman Lightsey (1914–19). The sheriffs typically appointed and supervised the jailers.

Shortly thereafter, however, a new sheriff was elected, Charlie V. Thomas, who served from 1919 to 1936. A new jailer was appointed, and conditions in the jail began to improve. By 1920, improvements were slowly

Hampton County sheriff Judson H. Lightsey. *Courtesy of the* Hampton County Guardian *archives.*

being made, and the new county officials added more space; better facilities, such as running water and, later, proper toilets; and generally more humane conditions. Wood-burning stoves were used for heat, and a few flushing toilets were added. By 1925, state officials wrote that, with a few more improvements, the jail would be one of the best in the state.

More improvements were made in the 1960s, but by the 1970s, the old jail had outlived its usefulness and a new jail was under construction. In 1976, the new facility in Varnille began taking inmates.

The former jail was then leased by Hampton County to the South Carolina Department of Wildlife and Marine Resources until 1989.

Since its nomination in 2011, the Hampton County Jail has been listed in the National Register of Historic Places. Still owned by the county, the former jail was converted to a museum by the Hampton County Historical Society. The second story was closed to the public in 2009 for structural safety reasons.

Now known as the Hampton County Museum @ The Old Jail, what was once a central place of wickedness in our county is now a center for education and historical preservation for future generations in Hampton County and the surrounding Lowcountry.

To learn more about the museum and the historical society, go to https://www.hchssc.org.

RACISM, CIVIL RIGHTS AND THE CONFEDERATE LEGACY

*W*hile Hampton County doesn't have the landmark historical significance of Selma, Alabama, or the site of the Orangeburg Massacre here in South Carolina, its history of racism has been no less virulent and violent. Our fair county has seen its share of racial violence, mob lynchings, and general institutionalized racism. The newspapers of days gone by are filled with tragic and angering accounts of racial injustice, with even the past editors of the *Hampton County Guardian* displaying the racist attitudes common in that era, referring to local Black residents as "Negroes," "coloreds" and worse.

Lynching and Vigilante Justice

With Reconstruction over, and federal protection gone, Hampton County became a violent and treacherous landscape for Black residents in the late 1800s and early 1900s. Crimes by Black residents were often punished by vigilante death, especially if they involved white victims. Just the perception of wrongdoing was enough to bring harsh punishment without the benefit of judge and jury. One vigilante incident involved the "world-famous" Brunson Town Hall.

The claim to fame of the tiny town of Brunson, located in the northern part of Hampton County, is its old town hall, built in 1906. The original town hall was cited in *Ripley's Believe It or Not!* as being the only octagonal-shaped town hall building in the world to be erected on stilts. The building served as a meeting place, recreational spot and voting place and was even the scene of an Election Day slaying until it was retired as a town hall in 1996. (The building now serves as the Brunson Museum and Visitors Center.)

The town hall was built on stilts to provide shade for the community's artesian well and as a popular gathering place for the locals. In September 1921, two young Black boys, Will Rodd and Sunny Best, were told in no uncertain terms that it was best for them to stay away, as it was a place for white people to congregate.

Rodd reportedly said that he would sit there if he wanted to and had a pistol if anyone tried to stop him.

The youths were promptly arrested for making threats. Around midnight, a white party came for them, took them to a nearby swamp and severely whipped them. None of the assailants were identified, even though the mob "made no pretense of masking themselves."

The headline in the *Guardian* read, "Whites Punish Insolent Negro." Other headlines, often written in the crude and insensitive fashion of that era, leave a horrible, telling record of our ancestors' ideas of justice for capital crimes like murder or rape.

A December 16, 1914, headline read, "Determined Men Slay Negro Brute: Jail Entered and Would-Be Rapist Taken Out and Shot to Death." Allen Seymour, a Black man in the employ of "gypsies" who were touring the county, was accused of attempting to criminally assault a young white girl living about four miles from Hampton. Seymour had been taken from the county jail about 1:00 a.m. by a mob of about forty or fifty men. His body was found about 1:00 p.m. the next day lying in a back road near Hampton. It appeared from evidence at the scene that the mob had turned him loose and allowed him to run, then pumped between eight and ten bullets into his head and body. During the following investigation, no one was able to identify any of the men in the mob.

The February 27, 1918, issue of the *Guardian* describes how between fifty and sixty white men from Fairfax lynched a local Black man named Walter Best, who was charged with killing a white auto shop owner in a drunken dispute over an automobile. County sheriffs were taking Best to the Barnwell County Jail to avoid angry locals when the mob stopped the transport, took the prisoner, strung him to a tree and a "good many shots were fired at him."

The local justice system worked differently for some of the white citizens. In February 1915, R.R. Peeples, a prominent white Estill resident, was acquitted of shooting to death Mary Jenkins, a Black woman roughly seventy years old. The acquittal came even though a seventeen-year-old white eyewitness testified that he "very positively" saw Peeples shoot the elderly woman without cause and despite Peeples giving contradictory statements to police and then to the court. After the killing, Peeples had signed an affidavit swearing that he did have a pistol on the day of the murder but did not take it out of his pocket. On the stand during the trial, however, he testified that he did not have a pistol.

Mack Johnson, a young white man living in Nixville during that era, had a dubious distinction: he was reportedly the first white man in Hampton County history to be convicted for killing a Black person. Johnson was convicted in February 1923 of manslaughter and carrying a concealed weapon for killing a Black man the previous December (the article doesn't name the victim). He was sentenced to twelve years, to be served at hard labor on the county chain gang or in the state penitentiary.

THE KU KLUX KLAN

Like almost everywhere in the Deep South, there was a local faction of the Ku Klux Klan in the Hampton County area. However, the Klan's visible presence tended to come and go over the decades, likely in response to certain events or changing times.

The September 26, 1925, edition of the *Guardian* documented "one of the largest crowds ever in county" attending a Klan rally in Fairfax, a tiny town that straddles Hampton and Allendale Counties.

An estimated crowd of 1,500 people attended the Thursday night parade and "naturalization ceremonies" staged by members of the Ku Klux Klan in "one of the most spectacular events ever staged in this section," wrote the *Guardian*.

The parade of about two hundred robed members from all over the state was headed by twelve of the leaders, who were mounted on robed horses. Three burning crosses were carried by different members, adding much to the effect of the scene.

Speeches were made by various members, and eleven new members were publicly initiated into the order, which is very strong in this section, wrote the paper. After the rally, the Klansmen were treated to refreshments that included cold drinks and sandwiches by the local ladies in attendance.

The Klan went silent for years, at least publicly, and then a June 1, 1949, *Guardian* report detailed how the Klan "paraded through this section," visiting Hampton, Varnville, Estill and Brunson. A forty-car motorcade of Klan members, led by the Grand Dragon's automobile equipped with sirens and a fiery cross (lit electrically), circled downtown Hampton and drove down Lee Avenue.

In late March 1960, a rash of cross burnings was held in various sections of the county. Four crosses were found in various parts of Estill and Scotia one Saturday night, and a three-by-five-foot cross was burned in the old ballpark lot in Hampton's West End section that same night. Hampton police told the *Guardian* they did not know who was responsible.

THE CONFEDERATE LEGACY

Hampton County, a place named after a Confederate general, did not part ways with its Confederate history easily or quickly.

The Custodians of Crosses of Honor of the Southern Association of the United Daughters of the Confederacy did not stop putting crosses of honor on the graves of Hampton County Confederate veterans until 1912. But in March of that year, a committee was formed to raise a Confederate monument in Hampton, the month before a monument was erected in Charleston to that "noble chieftain," General Wade Hampton. Even as late as 1939, amid news from the European front of World War II, there were headlines like "First Shot Is Celebrated," marking the seventy-eighth anniversary of the firing of the first shot in the "War Between the States" by a battery of Citadel cadets.

The March 25, 1936, issue of the *Guardian* reported the mournful occasion when Hampton County's last living Confederate veteran, Captain Preston Phillips, passed away at the age of ninety-two.

Hampton banker R.O. Bowden, known as an eccentric and rebellious character, drew nationwide attention for flying the Confederate flag high on the façade of his bank. On July 27, 1949, the *Guardian* reported that Bowden, president of the Loan and Exchange Bank of Hampton, had been showered with letters and cards of praise, as well as condemnation and surprise, from around the country after the widespread publication of an *Associated Press* photo of his Confederate flag bank decorations. He even received a letter from a past president of the United Daughters of the Confederacy commending him on his "spirit."

In the late 1960s, the Hampton County Watermelon Festival parade got off to a bang when a Civil War centennial float entitled "Forget Heck"

A gathering of Hampton County Confederate veterans, their wives and widows and United Daughters of the Confederacy members at Brunson High School, around 1908–10. *Courtesy of the* Hampton County Guardian *archives.*

exploded while the replica cannon was shooting off fireworks along the parade route. The Hampton Volunteer Fire Department promptly pulled out of the parade, caught up with the burning unit and doused the flames, preventing a serious fire and injuries to those on the float.

Civil Rights and Integration

Like most locations around the Jim Crow South, segregation was deeply ingrained in the fabric of Hampton County life. Churches and schools were segregated. There was a white local union and one for Black citizens in the county's largest factory, Plywood Plastics (later known as Westinghouse). Different races sat in separate locations to watch movies, and every public swimming pool in the county was "whites only." Black residents feared using the local hospital, and there were different waiting rooms at the local medical offices. You can visit many doctor and dentist offices in the Hampton area today and find that there are two front doors, often side by side or feet apart—one entrance and waiting room was once "whites only." Even women felt some discrimination; female residents weren't allowed to serve on a Hampton County jury until 1967.

VIOLENT UPRISINGS

During the 1960s and '70s, there were frequent claims of civil rights violations, from complaints involving the local hospital to employers to police officers. There were civil rights marches here, including one in December 1966 in downtown Hampton

In early 1968, Hampton County was rocked by a wave of arsons and violence. Four Black homes were burned, and in one incident, a Black man was injured by gunshots. In the April 10, 1968, edition of the *Guardian*, Hampton mayor Charles M. Boyles voiced shock and dismay at the racial outbreak that happened over the previous weekend and appealed to citizens of all races to "exercise restraint to avoid anything at all that might lead to misunderstanding and trouble between races."

The same week, county officials enacted a countywide curfew, restricting the hours of 8:00 p.m. to 5:00 a.m. to "protect life and property." Businesses were asked to close early, and only emergency traffic was allowed on the street. The curfew stayed in effect until April 20.

According to one local historian, the powerful but often notorious solicitor Randolph "Buster" Murdaugh Jr. didn't like having trouble in his hometown and made clandestine deals behind closed doors with both local Black leaders and the Klan to restore the peace. Reportedly, the out-of-town Klan members left the county, leaving just the local racists here to settle down on their own.

ELECTIONS AND VOTER RIGHTS

As people around the country fought for equal civil rights, there were others who worked against them. Voter suppression was one key to halting progress. During the civil rights era, there were numerous allegations of violations in our county, including claims that Black persons were being refused registration to vote.

In 1960, special agents of the Federal Bureau of Investigation and the U.S. Attorney's Office visited Hampton to examine and audit voter registration books

"The federal government and the FBI better be looking into what the Russians are doing instead of trying to run little Hampton County's business," a circuit judge, Judge T.B. Greneker, was quoted as saying.

A civil rights sit-in protest that included Notre Dame students and local activists at the old Hampton County Jail in 1969. *Photo courtesy of Peter J. McInerney and the* University of Notre Dame Class of 1969 Blog.

As in other places, there were civil rights marches here, along with election protests. It would take a major effort by the NAACP and "out of town instigators," as they were often called, to help turn the tide for local civil rights activists and Black voters.

In the late 1960s, students from three northern universities, Notre Dame, Saint Mary's and Holy Cross Junior College, made several journeys to Hampton County to organize and help its Black citizens register to vote while overcoming voter-suppression tactics. Once on the ground in Hampton County, they joined forces with members of the Hampton County Chapter of the NAACP, led by a dynamic local activist, James A. Moore. Moore, an ex-Marine of the famed Montford Point Marines, was president of the local chapter.

The Notre Dame students and other northern activists were soon met with open arms by Black citizens on both sides of the county. They opened their homes, businesses, and churches to them. The students were not greeted so kindly by many white citizens or officials in power. One local judge called them all communists in open court. They did not receive favorable coverage in the *Guardian*, either. Instead, Tom O'Connor, the editor at the time, wrote a March 22, 1967 front-page editorial:

> *Elsewhere in this issue, we carry a news story of some visitors to our county, to whom we cannot extend the hospitality usually accorded to strangers. For it is our belief that these visitors are here for the sole purpose of causing trouble, creating ferment and to try to give a peaceable people some unfavorable publicity.*

Ostensibly the visitors, we are hard put to find a name for them since they are neither here nor there, are in this county to force Negroes, who hitherto have felt no need of it, to register as voters.

Negroes in this county have no difficulty registering. So far as an honest effort to find the truth can discover, they have been welcome to register, whenever the books have been opened by law, and none qualified has been turned away.

The best way to handle a situation of this kind is to sit tight. Ignore the visitors. Let them go about their business, if it can be so called, in peace.

We are going to have to trust the sound common sense of our Negro friends to uncover the true intent of this drive and to determine that they will have no part of anything which can disrupt our peaceful lives together in this community.

Do not play their game, do not give them one chance to call in the television cameras, the Huntley-Brinkley types and other seekers of sensationalism. Stay away from them. In most cases the youths brought into the South on these drives are mixed up beings, more to be pitied than censured. They are dupes, manipulated by masters of forces of evil intent.

Let them have their fun on Saturday night and pray that they will soon find better things to do with lives they now waste.

One Notre Dame student activist, Peter McInerney, recorded the experiences in two articles. He wrote a short article for *Scholastic Magazine*'s May 3, 1968, issue, "The Good, the Bad, and the Ugly in Hampton County." Years later, he wrote a more detailed article for *The University of Notre Dame Class of 1969 Blog*, "A Call to Justice—Hampton County, South Carolina."

In these articles, McInerney described a "face-off" at the Hampton County Jail in April 1969 between local law-enforcement officials and voting rights marchers in the wake of several recent arrests. The articles also described the rural conditions, the poverty and the resistance to change. One Notre Dame student recalled meeting an old Black woman who was sitting in a creaking rocking chair on an old, splintered porch, "to watch the young give up on Hampton, to watch things go on as they have."

"I'm too old to be whipped anymore," she told the northern students.

The 1968 voter registration effort ended with a memorial march organized by Moore in memory of Dr. Martin Luther King Jr., who had recently been assassinated. The march drew between 350 and 500 participants. The route went directly, but peacefully, past the reputed headquarters of the local KKK, which was reported by McInerney to be located in a Pure brand

Civil rights protestors marching in Hampton County. *Courtesy of Peter J. McInerney and the* University *of Notre Dame Class of 1969 Blog.*

gas station. (A local historian has confirmed that this location was a Klan meeting place during that era.)

As a side note, during that time, Buster Murdaugh had his office across the street from the KKK headquarters and a liquor store next door. Local tongues wagged that this was so that he could keep an eye on the Klan, and if you needed to find a fella in trouble, the town liquor store was the place to do it.

The final memorial march of April 1969 did not go as peacefully. Roughly 250 people, including children, marched for one mile carrying signs demanding better jobs, recreation facilities and welfare benefits. But during the event, several protestors were arrested for blocking a roadway or resisting officers. Among those arrested were three of the leaders: James Moore; his son Michael Moore; and Carolyn Blake, the head of the NAACP Youth Group. Worried wife and mother Elizabeth Moore was summoned to the jail in hopes of posting bail for her husband and son but was refused entry and, in the process, elbowed in the face by a police officer, according to the Notre Dame history blog.

With their local leaders in jail, McInerney wanted to continue to protest while preventing violence. He led the marchers to the jail, where they sat on the public sidewalks for a silent "sit-in" until the NAACP could determine its next move.

The situation then escalated, and soon the Hampton town police were joined by the Hampton County Sheriff's deputies, the state highway patrol and Fourteenth Circuit solicitor Buster Murdaugh. Later, state officials arrived, including the governor and officers of the state police and the state

Above: Standoff with police at the Hampton County Jail. *Courtesy of Peter J. McInerney and the* University of Notre Dame Class of 1969 Blog.

Left: Civil rights march in Estill, southern Hampton County. *Courtesy of Peter J. McInerney and the* University of Notre Dame Class of 1969 Blog.

bureau of investigation. Tension grew, and police began producing riot gear. The protest leaders were told that if violence ensued, the authorities would charge the Notre Dame students with crossing state lines with intent to incite a riot.

The sit-in lasted six hours. During that time, the students sent people to a nearby restaurant to buy food, but they were denied service, so they contacted the FBI to file discrimination charges against the Hampton business.

Around 5:30 p.m., NAACP attorneys were able to arrange the release of everyone except Michael Moore, who had been charged with resisting and remained in jail, his bail set at $5,000. With most of their leaders freed, the group attempted to march back to their assembly point a mile away when a local youth tried to disrupt the return march by driving his car recklessly through their ranks. The suspect was arrested and charged with reckless driving and assault with intent to kill, but luckily, no one was seriously injured.

The students returned to their college community, leaving behind many encouraged and motivated Hampton County voters and soon-to-be voters. James A. Moore would continue to lead his community until 2012, when he died just six days after receiving the Congressional Gold Medal in Washington, D.C., for being one of the first African Americans to serve in the United States Marine Corps.

SCHOOL SEGREGATION

At one time in our county's history, there were scores of public school districts, often just one-room schoolhouses located in each community. And all of them were segregated by color.

They were separate but not equal. A January 1934 report by the South Carolina Department of Education found the state of "Negro schools" in Hampton County to be "very poor." Of the thirty-six Black schools, two weren't even running, and the sanitary and safety conditions in the rest were among the worst in the state. Only ten had sanitary toilets, some had crumbling walls or roofs and many did not have a heater or wood to burn in the winter.

Consolidation among schools of the same race took place over many years, and it wasn't until May 1951 that the number of county school districts was consolidated from sixteen down to two.

Amid threats of losing federal funding, public notices of the impending forced integration began running in the *Guardian* in early 1966. During the same period, the paper ran many editorials and guest columns opposing integration.

In July 1967, Hampton County School District One was cited as one of three districts in the state in danger of losing federal funding because of accusations of violating the Civil Rights Act of 1965. Hampton County public schools were not officially and fully integrated until 1970.

In January 1969, Hampton General Hospital announced that it was fully integrated and, in April of that year, was found to be in compliance with the Civil Rights Act of 1964.

To this day, the remains of many segregated schools, including historically important Rosenwald Schools, can be found in the area. One such school in Hampton now serves as "The Old Colored School" Museum. To learn more, go to https://www.hamptonsc.gov/hampton-colored-school-museum-and-resource-center.

GRISLY MURDERS STAIN THE PAGES OF HISTORY

The devil is never dead.... You fellows can take me out of here and kill me now.
—Unnamed Hampton man who tried to kill his wife and children
with an axe, May 1933

Since the Old Testament days of Cain and Abel, murder has been a common but powerful occurrence in human history, wrecking lives, destroying families and impacting communities. Rage, insanity and death are constant, shadowy companions that always reside in the human soul, hiding away in the dark recesses of our minds, waiting at any moment to slip the bounds of our self-control and explode into our lives.

Murder has taken many shapes and forms over the years in Hampton County, from the hate-filled, greed-inspired and premeditated killings to seemingly innocent moments erupting in anger-fueled violence. Murders have occurred in dark, swampy corners of the county and in broad daylight on Main Street and even, as we have seen, at the county courthouse. Homicides have happened in pool halls and drinking-filled roadside juke joints, as well as in churches and, on at least one occasion, on the way home from church, as evident in this unlikely story from the August 22, 1879, issue of the *Hampton County Guardian*.

It was a seemingly harmless situation. Joe Woods, G.C. Butch Owens and their families were on their way home from a revival at Sand Hill Church, near Cummings. No doubt, at least some of them were still filled with the Holy Spirit from the day's sermon and were humming Baptist hymns as the mule plodded along, pulling the wagons home. The day was hot, as August usually is in the South Carolina Lowcountry, but they were only about two miles from home, near Cummings, when tempers flared and trouble struck.

Joe Woods was driving the buggy owned by Owens, and when Owens's mule got tired and stopped, Woods began whipping the mule and cursing it. Irritated, Owens asked Woods to stop whipping his mule and cursing in front of Mrs. Owens, who was in the wagon just ahead with Mrs. E.W. Wells.

Woods apparently took this as a joke, and again the curses flew, even louder this time, and the whip cracked harder. Then Owens began to curse. At this point, Joe Woods and his brother Lee decided it was best for them to dismount the wagons and walk home to Cummings. But it was too late.

There was another exchange of curses, and an enraged Owens pulled his pistol and shot Joe Woods. According to testimony given at the coroner's inquest held the following Monday morning by Magistrate H.S. Koth, the victim staggered backward but was caught by Lee. Less than a minute later, Joe died in his brother's arms, blood staining the Sunday-go-to-meeting clothes of both men.

Picture this idyllic scene on Lee Avenue in April 1933: Two teenagers playing marbles in the dirt in front of the popular main street general store owned by Mayor J.F. Rivers. Nearby, a lazy old dog slept, not even looking up as the occasional Model A or Ford Deuce rumbled by. From time to time a customer would stop by to purchase a Coca-Cola or a block of ice.

It sounds like quite a quaint scene of yesteryear, a nostalgic moment in a small southern town. Well, it was, until a dispute over some stolen marbles sparked one angry teen to strike the other over the head with a stick, causing massive trauma to the brain. The fifteen-year-old boy died shortly after.

There have been many murders in Hampton County's history, some sparked by brief, angry encounters such as these that often led to a lifetime of regret, while others are more sinister and diabolical. Here are just a few of the worst murders in our county's history, including some crimes that made headlines around the state.

A WOMAN SCORNED?

At the little village of Fetchtig, Walker Winn clerked in the store of Mrs. Ella Wheeler Wells. It seems that the young man did not get along well with his young wife, Lillian Winn, and they had separated.

On the afternoon of September 17, 1910, Winn was suddenly taken ill. When medical aid arrived, it was found that he had symptoms of acute indigestion and apoplexy. The pupils of his eyes were widely dilated; soon afterward, he died. One witness reported that Winn clutched his side, said, "Oh, Ella, I'm dying!" and then went blind before losing consciousness.

"The tragic death of Walker Winn created quite a sensation in this section of the country," reported the *Guardian*.

After inquiring into the cause of death, the coroner's jury recommended that the contents of the stomach be analyzed.

By then, the body of young Winn was found to have turned black.

The coroner's jury considered the case for six months and finally rendered the verdict that the deceased came to his death from mercury poisoning administered by a person or persons unknown to the jurors. An analysis of the intestines and stomach contents revealed the presence of twelve milligrams of mercuric chloride, which was sufficient to cause death.

Of course, the hostile wife was immediately a suspect.

At the inquest on September 19, one of the witnesses testified that Winn's wife had asked of his whereabouts and then stated that "it was a wonder her father had not shot him and that she soon hoped to hear of her husband's death."

But investigators soon found that there were motives more powerful than scorned love: greed. Rumors began circulating around the county that Winn had his life insured in Mrs. Wells's favor for $1,000 and that she had collected the money.

In February 1912, Wells and an accomplice, Owen Robinson, were arrested, charged with Winn's murder and deposited in the Hampton County Jail. The warrant of arrest was issued by Magistrate J.G. Murdaugh of Hampton, on an affidavit by Lizzie Terry, mother of the deceased young man.

THE BODY ON THE TRACKS

During the week of September 12, 1928, Randolph Murdaugh Sr. prosecuted a murder case that packed the Hampton County Courthouse but didn't take long to unravel.

Joe Brown, of Hampton, was charged in the death of James Mauldin, whose "crushed and torn body" was found on the railway tracks of the Charleston and Western Carolina Railway in Hampton early that previous Monday morning.

Numerous witnesses were examined by Solicitor Murdaugh Monday night before a courtroom full of curious and concerned citizens. Among those witnesses was the engineer of the freight train, who testified that he was positive there was no body on the tracks when his train arrived at that location. No blood was found at the scene, and Eugene M. Peeples, the Hampton undertaker who had taken possession of the body, testified that there was hardly a pint of blood left in the corpse.

Other evidence gathered by the coroner's inquest seemed to point to the fact that young Mauldin had been murdered and his body thrown between the boxcars of the early morning freight train. It was clear that the victim had been killed elsewhere and his body thrown on the tracks to make the death appear accidental.

Other witnesses testified that Mauldin and some of his friends were at a party when a disagreement broke out between him and Brown, during which Brown beat Mauldin with his belt. The two rivals were later seen going at it at a filling station after midnight.

It didn't take the jury long to reach a verdict.

TEENAGER KILLS PARENTS

One of the most heartbreaking cases in county history involved a Cummings teenager who killed both of his parents.

Charles H. Mixon Jr., seventeen, a ninth-grade student at Varnville High School, was charged with the murder of his father, Charles Mixon, and mother, Jennie Patience Mixon, on the Wednesday afternoon of February 22, 1951. The killings took place about sundown.

The bodies were found Thursday night by a married daughter, Argual Barnes, and her husband, who had come to visit. The mother's body was found in a bedroom closet. The father's body was found later in an outhouse.

The schoolboy was arrested very early Friday morning by Sheriff Alton M. Lightsey and was taken to the Hampton County Jail. He admitted shooting his parents with a .22-caliber rifle. The boy showed officers where he dragged the body of the father after shooting him as he entered the lot gate, returning from plowing a field.

Mixon was ordered to be committed to the South Carolina State Hospital on Bull Street in Columbia on February 26 on Solicitor Randolph "Buster" Murdaugh Jr.'s recommendation and a court order signed by Judge Frank E. Eaton. He was then transferred to the state mental hospital by Deputy Sheriff H.C. Mixon for thirty days of mental observation. The hospital's findings were to be reported to Murdaugh and Clerk of Court B.T. DeLoach.

As the legal and mental health systems went to work, about one thousand people were present at the double funeral on Saturday, February 24, at Sand Hill Baptist Church. The victims had three other children, all daughters.

After the thirty-day observation, Mixon was found to be "without mental disorders." The opinion of the hospital staff was that seventeen-year-old Mixon was in quite good physical condition but functioned psychologically on the level of a much younger child. According to the state's doctors, he was "dull normally but not deficient, had no evidence of a psychosis and shows no mental disorder."

Neither court records nor newspaper accounts gave any indication as to the circumstances leading up to the killings or any possible motive.

Mixon was returned to the Hampton County Jail to await trial in June. Because of extensive family relationships in the county, it was difficult to find an eligible jury. Even a new clerk of court had to be sworn in for the trial, because B.T. DeLoach was related to the family and had to be excused.

During early June 1951, Mixon was tried initially for only his father's murder. During the trial, testimony indicated that the boy admitted to Deputy Sheriff H.C. Mixson that he killed both of his parents. Dr. G.B. Carrigan, senior assistant physician at the state hospital, testified that the boy was judged sane but was considered "subnormal" mentally, having the mind of an eleven-year-old.

A Hampton County jury returned a guilty verdict but with a recommendation for mercy so the boy could be spared the death penalty. Judge J. Henry Johnson handed down a sentence of life to be served either on the Hampton County Public Works chain gang or in the state penitentiary.

With this outcome, Mixon's attorney, state senator Brantley Harvey of Beaufort, entered a guilty plea in the killing of the mother, and Mixon also received a life sentence for that murder.

THE CASE OF THE ESTILL BASEBALL BAT SLAYER

One of the most horrific and shocking crimes in South Carolina Lowcountry history occurred in the quiet town of Estill, located in southern Hampton County, and involved victims who were brutalized by someone they should have loved and trusted: the patriarch of the family.

The murderer, John D. Bowers, an Estill storekeeper, had been described in many ways, including being insane. "Alright when he wasn't drinking" was another description.

Guilty, Gets Life Imprisonment

Midnight Verdict Ends Jurors' 7-Hour Deliberation

JOHN BOWERS

Court Acts On 19 Cases

The Court of General Sessions, Judge James Woodrow Lewis, of

John D. Bowers, 43-year old Estill baseball bat slayer was sentenced to life imprisonment by Judge James Woodrow Lewis after the jury returned a verdict of guilty with recommendation of mercy at 12:27 a. m. Thursday.

The jury had been deliberating since 4:40 p.m. Wednesday, returning once at 10: 15 p.m. to hear the court stenographer read the medical testimony.

Bowers, former Estill store keeper, sat stony-faced throughout the trial and exhibited no emotion when the verdict was read.

The court room was jammed Wednesday morning and afternoon and was still half-filled when the verdict was read early Thursday morning.

Indicted on three counts of murder, he was tried on only one - -the killing of his three-and-half year old daughter Sandra on the evening of December 8, 1948. He clubbed his wife, Mae Phillips Bowers, and seven-year-old son Wayne, to death with a baseball bat at the same

licitor showed him the bat Lindsey said it was the weapon in the killings.

The sheriff said Bowers med him shortly after the that he killed his wife an girl second and then "He said the boy was ki kill than the girl," the said. Lindsey testified questioned at that tim could distinguish bet and wrong.

The first defense E. P. Ellis, judge who testified that been committed to pital twice in 1944 to the records i office had never ced sane by the

B T DeLoach, testified that

A news clipping depicting the horrific family murder case involving John Bowers of Estill. *Courtesy of the* Hampton County Guardian *archives.*

Bowers had been committed to the state mental hospital twice in 1944, but county records show that, although released, he had never been "pronounced sane," the papers of the day reported.

On what newspaper accounts describe as a "gloomy night" in the normally quiet town of Estill, Bowers murdered his wife, son and daughter in a particularly violent and gruesome fashion, yet with a premeditated calmness that is chilling.

Bowers used his son's baseball bat to beat to death his wife, Mae Phillips Bowers, thirty-eight; daughter Sandra, four; and son Wayne, seven, at their Estill home on the evening of December 8, 1948.

He killed the wife first and then the children. A neighbor later testified that he heard the sound of children crying and a dog barking, then a noise like a sledgehammer hitting something.

The triple homicide made headlines as far away as Sioux Falls, South Dakota. The *Daily Argus-Leader* reported that Bowers had "calmly" confessed to Fourteenth Circuit solicitor Randolph "Buster" Murdaugh Jr.

that he had waited for his family to return home from a movie and then turned on them one by one because, he said, he and his wife had not been "getting along as well."

On December 10, 1948, two days after the killings, Bowers was admitted to the South Carolina State Hospital in Columbia, or "Bull Street," as state residents often called it. Admitting its first patient in 1828 as the South Carolina Lunatic Asylum, it was one of the first public mental hospitals established in the United States and has quite a dark history of its own.

Bowers was placed there for observation by court order of Circuit Judge Steve Griffin of Newberry. A month later, on January 10, 1949, Dr. W.P. Beckman, acting superintendent of the hospital, informed Solicitor Murdaugh by letter that his medical staff had diagnosed Bowers as insane.

However, even though this was Bowers's third commitment to the mental hospital, in a follow-up letter dated June 21, 1950, Dr. Beckman informed Murdaugh that medical authorities believed Bowers had "recovered from mental illness" and should be remanded to the court for further disposition.

Dr. Beckman further informed Murdaugh that Bowers suffered from "alcoholic psychosis—acute hallucinosis" and warned that "Bowers is considered a dangerous person in that, if he returned to society and resumed the use of alcohol he would probably react in a similar manner."

Interviewed in Hampton, Murdaugh told the *Hampton County Guardian* that he and Sheriff Lightsey had done everything in their power to have Bowers kept at the state hospital but added that the murder trial would be "just another case to me" and he would ask the jury to give Bowers "the chair and nothing less."

On the news that Bowers was being released from the mental hospital and returning to Hampton County for trial, the community of Estill was in such a state of renewed grief that on July 5 of that year Estill mayor C.F. Brewton and the Estill Town Council adopted a resolution on the matter. The resolution stated: "The terrifying slayings that took place on a gloomy night here when Mrs. Bowers, Sandra and Wayne were coming home from the matinee are still as fresh in the minds of Estill citizens as the night it happened. It was the feeling of practically everyone here, and certainly of the town authorities, that Bowers should not be released from the state hospital."

The town sent copies of the resolution to the solicitor, the sheriff and the county legislative delegation, requesting that Bowers be kept in the hospital, but if he was released that a speedy trial be arranged.

This effort would prove in vain. John Bowers, father of a murdered family, was coming home to Hampton County.

A HEART-WRENCHING TRIAL

The trial was slated for the October 1950 term of court in Hampton County General Sessions, and it would be a painful, albeit well-attended one. Throughout the emotional trial, witnesses produced heart-wrenching testimony, while Bowers, forty-three at the time, sat "stony-faced" throughout the proceedings and "exhibited no emotion" when the verdict was finally read, reported one local paper.

Indicted on three charges of murder, Bowers was tried on only one that day, the killing of his four-year-old daughter, Sandra. He had entered a plea of not guilty to all three indictments.

The trial was covered by two area newspapers, the *Hampton County Guardian* and *Hampton County Democrat*.

Prior to the trial, Murdaugh told the *Democrat* that, while the case was "one of the most sensational in this section of the country in recent years," he would treat it just like any other murder case and would seek the death penalty. Murdaugh added that he would seek the death penalty on the grounds that "the temporary insanity" under which Bowers bludgeoned three members of his family to death was the result of Bowers's "voluntary excessive use of alcohol."

The October 25, 1950, issue of the *Guardian* reported that the one-day trial began at 9:30 a.m. on a Wednesday and ended in a red-eye jury verdict just before 1:00 a.m. Thursday. The trial itself did not last long, but the jury selection took hours—court officials had to extend their search beyond the five-mile radius for willing and eligible jurors—and the jury deliberation took roughly eight hours.

Solicitor Murdaugh based his case on the assertion that the defendant could distinguish between right and wrong at the time of the killings. The defense's attorney attempted to prove that Bowers was not sane and not legally responsible.

Dr. Johnson Peeples, a noted Estill physician and the first witness for the state, told the court that he arrived at the Bowerses' residence shortly after the killings to find Mrs. Bowers and Wayne dead and Sandra still alive but with a crushed skull. The little girl lived for about an hour after being taken to the Ridgeland, South Carolina hospital.

When Buster Murdaugh exhibited the baseball bat, Sheriff Lightsey confirmed that it was the weapon used in the killings. Lightsey also gave the opinion that, when questioned upon arrest, Bowers could tell right from wrong. The sheriff then testified that Bowers, shortly after his arrest, confessed that he killed his wife first, the girl next and then the boy. "He said the boy was harder to kill than the girl," the sheriff testified grimly.

Dr. Carr T. Larisey, a well-known Hampton doctor, testified that after the arrest Bowers told him that someone was trying to kill him with "poison gas" and that "guns were being pointed at him from next door."

When asked about the children, Bowers confessed to Dr. Larisey that he killed them "just because they happened to be there." Another witness testified that the accused murderer didn't "show feelings you would expect in a normal person."

Otis Lightsey, a next-door neighbor, testified that between 6:00 p.m. and 6:30 p.m. that day he heard children crying and a dog barking, and then "for five or ten minutes I heard a noise like a sledgehammer hitting something."

Estill police chief Abe DeLoach, who was first on the scene, testified that the defendant walked out of his house with the bat in his hand and went to his brother K.S. Bowers's store.

"Blood was spattered seven-and-a-half feet up the living room walls," Chief DeLoach said on the stand.

One of Bowers's surviving older sons testified that he saw Bowers enter the store, bat in hand, and say, "I just killed my old lady." Another son told the court that his father had an "ungovernable temper," was "always raising hell" and had threatened to kill his wife "plenty of times," once with a pocketknife.

In his defense, attorney C.B. Searson claimed that the killings were done by "a crazy man."

"Could a sane man destroy his little girl and boy because of his wife?" he asked. "Poor John Bowers destroyed his family when he was in a condition for which he was not responsible. Give him a chance."

In his closing remarks, Buster Murdaugh said, "John Bowers has to be removed from society by electrocution if Hampton County is to be made a safe place in which to live." Murdaugh also told the jury, "If he is ever released on society and kills again, no one is responsible but yourselves."

The October 13 *Democrat* reported that the jury began deliberating around 4:40 p.m., returning once at 10:15 p.m. to hear the court stenographer read the medical testimony from two local doctors.

The courtroom was jammed with spectators that morning and still half full when the verdict was read after midnight.

It would be a shocking, disappointing verdict for some.

THE VERDICT

The twelve-man jury (women were not allowed to serve on Hampton County juries at that time) deliberated for nearly eight hours to deliver a verdict of guilty, with a "recommendation for mercy," in the murder of the preschool daughter, Sandra.

On October 12, 1950, Judge J. Woodrow Lewis of Darlington, South Carolina, sentenced Bowers to "be held to labor for the period of his natural lifetime in the state penitentiary." Bowers was transported to the penitentiary later the same day by deputies of the Hampton County Sheriff's Office.

The other two counts of murder—the deaths of Bowers's wife and son— were transferred to the court's contingent docket.

Murdaugh said that Bowers would not be eligible for parole until he had served at least ten years, and should he come up for parole, the parole board would have to hear recommendations from both the solicitor and the judge.

Bowers, now a man without a family or a home, was transferred to begin the first of many years in the South Carolina State Penitentiary in Columbia in Richland County. He would be sharing his new home with 1,450 other hardened, convicted criminals from around the state.

But Bowers's courtroom battles were far from over.

SEPARATED IN DEATH, AS IN LIFE

Bowers would make two more trips to his former home in Hampton County. In June 1961, he was convicted of a second count of murder and again sentenced to life imprisonment, to run consecutively to the first life sentence, by Judge William L. Rhodes. On October 10, 1961, Bowers was trice convicted of murder in the same court and sentenced to a third life sentence, to run concurrently with the first two, by Judge Steve C. Griffith.

Bowers filed a petition for a correction of sentences, and that petition was denied by Judge John Grimball on February 19, 1962.

The convicted murderer then filed an appeal that went all the way to the South Carolina Supreme Court. That appeal was denied on October 30, 1962.

Bowers died in Columbia, South Carolina, on March 7, 1979, at the age of seventy-three. Family genealogy records indicate that he is buried in the DeLoach Family Cemetery in Nixville, not far from his family's home in Estill.

Bowers's wife and their children Sandra and Wayne lie at rest at Beech Branch Baptist Church Cemetery in another county, Allendale.

Separated from his family in life by alcohol, violence, mental illness and prison, Bowers remains separated from his family in death.

RIPPED FROM THE HEADLINES

Hampton County Herald
January 4, 1917
Double Killing Near Brunson Last Friday
One of the most awful tragedies in the history of Hampton County occurred at the home of Mr. P.W. Lightsey, about six miles from the County Seat....

The double deaths occurred after H.A. Preacher, of Brunson, went out in his automobile with a tenant, Keb Nettles, along with two other tenants driving wagons, to secure and convey from P.W. Lightsey's farm some provisions claimed to have been left there by Nettles, who had formerly lived there. Lightsey was holding the provisions because he claimed that Nettles owed him some money.

Lightsey, anticipating the move by Preacher, and fearing trouble, telephoned Sheriff Lightsey, who also lived in Brunson, for protection. Sheriff Lightsey arrived with a deputy but failed to prevent Preacher and Nettles from entering the front yard.

Within a few paces of the front steps of the Lightsey residence, Preacher fell, riddled with buckshot after being shot twice, presumably with both barrels of a shotgun fired from the bedroom window. Quickly following those blast two more shots rang out and Nettles fell, riddled in a like manner.

Sheriff Lightsey reported the killings, and large numbers of citizens went to the scene and witnessed "two white citizens of Hampton County, one of considerable prominence, Mr. Preacher, lying dead in the yard," wrote the *Herald*. "The sad affair is greatly deplored and has cast a cloud of gloom over the entire neighborhood."

MOONSHINE, MURDER AND MURDAUGH MAYHEM

Hampton County, September 1910: An ambitious young lawyer explores politics, personal injury and prosecution, birthing a legal dynasty.

Charleston, 1956: The federal government goes after a powerful but allegedly corrupt prosecutor in a moonshine conspiracy case but can't bring him down.

Beaufort County, February 2019: There's a girl in the frigid, salty waters of Archers Creek, and a prominent family is involved. It takes search-and-rescue teams a week to recover her body, as the public screams for justice and answers.

Colleton County, June 2021: The young man police say is responsible for the girl's death lies shot to death at his family's vast rural estate. His mother lies murdered a short distance away. Soon, other crimes and homicides are exposed in a scandalous web that engulfs people around the South Carolina Lowcountry.

The tragic events surrounding the Murdaugh family of Hampton County have made headlines around the English-speaking world and will go down as one of most sensational criminal stories in South Carolina history. But the Murdaughs' legendary and controversial history is just as fascinating as these current events. There were wicked skeletons in this family's historical closet long before they first appeared on the cover of *People* magazine and on primetime television.

MURDAUGHS MAKE INTERNATIONAL HEADLINES

Spawned in the aftermath of the fallen Confederacy, the Murdaugh dynasty assumed legal and political power in lower South Carolina in 1910.

For more than one hundred years, the Murdaughs made legends of themselves in Hampton County and around the Fourteenth Judicial Circuit, a five-county area of the South Carolina Lowcountry that ranges from the world-class resorts of Hilton Head Island to the swamps of poor, rural Allendale County. For three generations, members of this family ran a massive personal-injury law firm that would eventually lead Hampton County to be labeled one of the worst "judicial hellholes" in the country. At the same time, Murdaughs ruled the criminal justice system. Three men named Randolph Murdaugh would serve as Fourteenth Circuit solicitor for eighty-five-plus years, the longest term of prosecutorial service of any family in U.S. history. For the better part of a century, the Randolph Murdaughs decided what cases were crimes, what crimes were to be punished and who deserved mercy, often without the need of judge and jury.

The Murdaughs were talented attorneys and fierce prosecutors, and their dynasty was a century of prominence and greatness in the courtroom. It was also a time of great controversy and alleged corruption.

The Murdaugh prosecutors built a network of connections, from lawyers, judges and senators to law-enforcement members and voting jurors. Amid the whispers of scandal and privilege, most locals either loved them or feared them, but few dared to oppose them, and the secrets of the Murdaugh legal dynasty were safeguarded within the confines of the Fourteenth Circuit—until a fateful night in 2019.

In the early hours of February 24, 2019, Paul Murdaugh, grandson of former Fourteenth Circuit solicitor Randolph III and youngest son of assistant solicitor and law partner Richard "Alex" Murdaugh, allegedly crashed his father's boat in Beaufort County waters while intoxicated. Five other teens were on board, including Mallory Beach, a nineteen-year-old college student from Hampton County, who went into the water and was found drowned a week later.

Because of the high-profile family involved and the notably shocking public fact that young Beach was missing in the river for a week, this case drew intense media and public interest. Some of the top investigative journalists in South Carolina, including the award-winning John Monk at the *State*, began digging into the Murdaugh family's history, eager to learn more about this fascinating family.

What were once Hampton County's dirty little secrets soon became a Palmetto State scandal reminiscent of the Ted Kennedy car crash incident of 1969.

On April 18, 2019, a grand jury indicted Paul Murdaugh on three felony charges related to the crash, including boating under the influence causing death. On May 6, Murdaugh pleaded not guilty to all charges and was released on bond. But he would never stand trial.

On the night of June 7, 2021, Paul and his mother, Margaret, were shot and killed at their vast Colleton County estate, Moselle.

Almost overnight, South Carolina's top crime story exploded, making international headlines and being featured on prime-time television. Movie and documentary companies came calling. True-crime authors began prowling the streets of once-quiet Hampton County.

Soon, allegations of other crimes would emerge, the world would learn about more unsolved deaths and more victims would cry out for justice as investigators discovered a dark side to the supposedly grieving father, Alex Murdaugh.

The world continued unraveling for Murdaugh in an alleged failed suicide-for-hire ploy over Labor Day weekend in 2021 after he was ousted from the law firm his great-grandfather founded. Within a year, Murdaugh was disbarred and facing more than one hundred criminal charges and a dozen civil suits in connection with a decade-long, multicounty drug and financial crime spree.

Then, on July 14, 2022, Murdaugh was charged with the murders of his wife and son and was jailed in the state capital on a $7 million bond while awaiting his many days in court.

The details behind the Murdaugh murder and crime saga were still coming to light in courtrooms around the state, but the world now knows much more about the history of this storied and controversial family of attorneys who ruled the Fourteenth Circuit for more than a century.

WHO ARE THE MURDAUGHS?

Murdaugh was a household name in Hampton County long before their story made headlines in the *New York Times* and was featured on *Dateline NBC*. While some in the tabloid media and social media have painted members of this family with a broad brush, alleging entitlement and corrupt cover-ups on every corner, there was much more to this family than that. There was greatness, talent and ambition, and local historians and journalists can rightfully argue that, for every alleged misdeed, there was a great deed and a contribution to their communities and to the law.

JOSIAH PUTNAM MURDAUGH II (1840–1912): CONFEDERATE HERO, WEALTHY BUSINESSMAN

From its beginnings, the Murdaugh family dynasty in South Carolina is gilded with an almost legendary southern mystique. This storied family doesn't just trace its roots back to the Confederacy; its legends also claim that their ancestors were right there rubbing elbows with General Robert E. Lee and Confederate president Jefferson Davis.

Alex Murdaugh's great-great-grandfather Josiah Putnam Murdaugh II (1840–1914) was the son of Josiah Putnam I and Mary Ursala Varn, who came from a noted local family for which the town of Varnville is named. According to the history *From the Salkehatchie to the Savannah*, J.P. II married Annie Marvin Davis, a first cousin of Jefferson Davis, the president of the Confederate States of America.

According to National Park Service records, Murdaugh was a member of an artillery battalion attached to the Hampton Legion, South Carolina, which was organized by Wade Hampton during the spring of 1861 and saw many battles and suffered a great number of casualties. General Hampton would become an important name in state and local history, as he would later become governor of the state and a powerful political force during Reconstruction. Hampton County and the town of Hampton, where the Murdaughs would later establish a law practice, were later named in his honor.

Hart's Company of South Carolina Horse Artillery Volunteers (also known as the Washington Light Artillery) was originally organized under Captain James F. Hart to be attached to the Hampton Legion but never officially served with that command, records the park service. After being stationed in South Carolina, the group moved to Virginia and fought with the Army of Northern Virginia from the Seven Days' Battles to Cold Harbor, then was involved in the Siege of Petersburg. The unit later joined an artillery unit with the Army of Tennessee and was active in North Carolina and then at Gettysburg before surrendering in April 1865.

After the war, J.P. Murdaugh II moved from Colleton County to Beaufort and from there to Charleston County, where he was successful in the phosphate mining and commercial fertilizer industries until the mid-1800s.

He amassed wealth in real estate development in Beaufort and Hampton Counties and was involved in at least one major land acquisition in Almeda, an unincorporated area near Varnville. Much of the "Almeda Tract," as it has been called, remains in the Murdaugh family.

In 1885, his eyesight failing, Murdaugh retired to the sleepy railroad town of Varnville, where he served as the moneylender for residents of Varnville and the Almeda area until his death.

The first Murdaugh home in Varnville burned in 1915, and J.P.'s widow, Anna Marvin Davis Murdaugh, would die four years later. Her obituary in the August 6, 1919 issue of the *Hampton County Guardian* noted that her birthplace was the beautiful estate Dorchester, so often mentioned by the author Gilmore Simms. It goes on to assert that she was distantly related to the "great and illustrious statesman" Jefferson Davis and was a "loyal daughter of the Confederacy" as well as a member of the Wade Hampton Chapter of the United Daughters of the Confederacy.

Mr. and Mrs. J.P. Murdaugh II had eight children, but only four survived their parents and only two remained in Hampton County.

RANDOLPH MURDAUGH SR.

(February 28, 1887–July 19, 1940):
Ambitious Lawyer, Fearless Prosecutor

The youngest son, Randolph Murdaugh Sr., was born in Varnville in 1887. With his family's wealth and connections at his back, young Murdaugh attended the U.S. Naval Academy and then graduated from the University of South Carolina in 1908 before finishing at the USC School of Law in 1910.

Three men would eventually bear the name Randolph Murdaugh, and while there were similarities, each one made a distinct mark on the family dynasty. But without a doubt, the first of the three Randolphs was the least controversial.

Fresh out of law school, this Murdaugh was out to make a name for himself in the field of law and launch a legal dynasty, and he wasted little time before opening his own practice, setting up shop as a one-man law firm in Hampton in 1910. According to Murdaugh family lore and local historians, Murdaugh never bothered to hang a sign outside his law office, and neither did his children or grandchildren, who also practiced law. Everyone knew where the Murdaugh firm was located.

Randolph Murdaugh Sr. in front of his home in Varnville, 1920s. *Courtesy of the* Hampton County Guardian *archives*.

Murdaugh's solo practice added partners over the decades, including his son, grandson and great-grandsons, and would grow to become one of the largest personal-injury law firms in the state. Four generations of Murdaughs eventually practiced law at what would come to be known as Peters Murdaugh Parker Eltzroth & Detrick, PA (PMPED).

Private practice wasn't enough for the ambitious lawyer, and in 1920, he ran for the office of solicitor of the five-county Fourteenth Judicial Circuit. Once again, local Murdaugh lore makes heavy claims that as a political contender no one ever dared oppose Randolph and that he ran "without ever having had opposition." Despite this claim—which has been repeated in his law firm and family histories and even in his obituary—he did face two political rivals in his first election of 1920 but easily won. Filing for the office against him were R.M. Jeffries and Heber R. Padgett, an attorney who would later work alongside Randolph to prosecute at least one major case.

At the time, there was no rule against circuit prosecutors serving as private-practice attorneys in South Carolina, so Murdaugh also enjoyed work at his lucrative practice. He also served as the town of Varnville's official attorney for twenty-five dollars a year while taking on criminal cases. In 1932, the *Columbia Record* described Solicitor Murdaugh as "one of the busiest lawyers in the lower state in civil practice."

MURDAUGH SR. AS A PROSECUTOR

While Murdaugh Sr. did not suffer from the same controversies that would surround his son and later generations of Murdaughs, he nevertheless made headlines in a spectacular fashion while prosecuting some wicked lawbreakers.

Randolph served on the Grievance Committee of the South Carolina Bar Association, and newspaper headlines paint the image of a fearless prosecutor who often targeted those in power, from bankers and preachers to sheriffs and a former governor, well beyond the humble reaches of small-time Hampton County.

Murdaugh Sr. took on cases involving officers of three of the largest banking institutions of that era in Hampton County, banks where he, his family and his associates likely did business. On September 21, 1926, the Hampton County Grand Jury asked the solicitor to hand down indictments on officers of the Merchants and Planters Bank of Varnville, the Merchants and Planters Bank of Brunson and the Bank of Hampton for violations of the state's banking laws.

In February 1928, Murdaugh Sr., working with Hampton attorney George Warren, earned convictions on two Beaufort County bankers for making false statements in a conspiracy scandal involving the former Beaufort Bank. The convictions were appealed to the South Carolina Supreme Court but were upheld.

Taking on bad bankers would even pull the Hampton attorney out of his power zone in the Fourteenth Circuit. In July 1930, he was appointed by South Carolina attorney general John M. Daniel to represent the state's interests during a special term of court in Lancaster, 149 miles away in the South Carolina Upstate. He prosecuted the case against two officers of the First National Bank and Trust, a defunct organization at that time, that had also been accused of violating state banking laws.

Murdaugh Sr. was prosecuting cases against bankers even though he was associated with and profited from his own banking ventures around the state. On November 13, 1928, an official grand opening statement of the Peoples Bank of Columbia listed the prosecutor on its board of directors. The bank was affiliated with numerous financial institutions around the state, including the Hampton Banking Company, which had two branches in Hampton County, at Varnville and Estill, and one in nearby Ehrhardt, South Carolina.

In May 1921, he was appointed a local representative of the First Carolinas Joint Stock Land Bank, a new corporation organized to loan money on improved farmlands as well as city property in the two Carolinas. The May 20 issue of the *Hampton County Guardian* stated that the corporation offered loans "with as little red tape in the matter as possible" and "with as great expedition as possible," adding that Mr. Murdaugh was ready at any time to interview those anticipating getting loans.

Today, prosecuting bankers while profiting from their competitors would likely be considered a conflict of interest.

In April 1921, Murdaugh Sr. took up a case against a Hampton County auditor, T. Hagood Gooding, in a hearing that went before South Carolina governor Robert Cooper. The auditor was accused of not complying with state tax commission mandates, such as supplying a complete list of Hampton County merchants, not properly assessing automobiles and not placing "on the books" stocks owned by local merchants. The newspaper further added that, in addition to numerous "expert witnesses," Murdaugh's case included "a wagon load of books, papers and records" taken from the auditor's and treasurer's office that were admitted into evidence.

During the week of September 28, 1922, at the request of Governor Wilson Harvey, Murdaugh Sr. prosecuted a case against Colleton County sheriff W.H. Ackerman, who was indicted by a Colleton County grand jury on charges of malfeasance in office concerning "shortages in the finances of his office." The shortages were reportedly from delinquent tax funds, but the accused sheriff had promised to make good on those missing funds.

During the week of September 12, 1928, the busy solicitor prosecuted a Hampton murder case that brought a packed courtroom. The case involved Joe Brown and his charge in the death of James Mauldin, covered in this book in chapter 11.

Murdaugh Sr. was also involved in two major cases with state-level implications, one in defense of a South Carolina governor and one in prosecution of a former governor.

During Allendale County General Sessions Court the week of July 11, 1924, he prosecuted a major case against former South Carolina governor Wilson G. Harvey, also the former president of the Enterprise Bank of Charleston, who was charged with violating state banking laws by accepting deposits even though he knew the failing bank was insolvent. The case pitted Murdaugh Sr. against another South Carolina legal legend, Edgar A. Brown of Barnwell, who would later become a powerhouse state senator and part of a powerful group of politicians known as the "Barnwell Ring." Judge J. Henry Johnson presided.

During the trial, Solicitor Murdaugh called five key witnesses and produced numerous banking documents. Over the strong objections of the defense, he placed the former governor in the prisoner's dock while the indictment was being read, likely in a subtle attempt to make him look guilty and possibly add insult to injury—an early example of the type of colorful, and often controversial, courtroom antics that his son and grandson would later become known for and often sanctioned for.

Set in Allendale, just thirty minutes away from Murdaugh's stronghold of Hampton and Brown's power base in Barnwell, the well-publicized trial resulted in an acquittal of Harvey, even though the defense called no witnesses, and its closing argument was simply that the prosecution had failed to produce enough evidence to convict its client.

During a later trial in Allendale, in April 1925, Murdaugh Sr. was able to earn a guilty plea from Harvey on charges of lending money to a corporation in which he had interests more than the amount allowed by law. The former governor pleaded guilty to lending excessive amounts of the Enterprise Bank's money to the Consolidated Truck and Auto Company of Charleston. In accepting Harvey's guilty plea, Solicitor Murdaugh agreed to drop two other charges that included Harvey allegedly giving excessive loans to himself and to his brother-in-law.

Judge John S. Wilson stated that, because of Harvey's previous clean record, he was sentencing him to either four months in prison or a $400 fine, after which Harvey immediately agreed to pay the fine.

The roles were reversed during an August 1931 appeal hearing before the South Carolina Supreme Court. Murdaugh Sr. represented Governor Ibra Blackwood after the governor removed Jasper County sheriff Ben F. Spivey from office. The sheriff had been removed after an alleged shortage in his accounts, but he claimed his ouster was politically motivated.

While cases involving governors and bankers made headlines statewide, one of Murdaugh Sr.'s most scandalously interesting cases was tried a little closer to home. On June 15, 1927, he helped convict a Pentecostal Holiness preacher charged with sexual assault.

In a trial that was described as "one of the most interesting and sensational ever held in Colleton County," a jury found the Reverend Lloyd M. Bishop guilty of statutory criminal assault after a short trial in Walterboro, South Carolina.

Reverend Bishop was charged with a crime against a young woman who lived near the town of Cottageville. In the courtroom was the girl as well as her baby boy. During the trial, the child played around on the floor of the courtroom, "the innocent cause of the legal battle which raged for two days," wrote the *Watchman and Southron* newspaper of Sumter.

Ivy A. Smoak, a probate judge, was appointed counsel for the accused preacher, while Murdaugh Sr. and Herber R. Padgett, once a political rival of Randolph's, represented the state.

According to statements presented during the trail, Bishop could not get along with the local Pentecostal Holiness church, so he and a coworker met one day, each baptizing the other, and founded their own church in Colleton County to teach and preach the Holiness doctrine.

It was also stated that the father of the scandalized female was friendly to Bishop and had erected a Holiness chapel near his home, and "there sprang up great intimacy between the two families, and much visiting resulted," wrote the Sumter paper.

During testimony, it was stated that Bishop had "won the confidence" of the girl, who was between the ages of thirteen and fourteen at the time, and appointed her as one of his assistants before later licensing her to preach. From this intimacy grew the illicit relationship that resulted in the birth of the child, Murdaugh and Padgett contended.

The young woman testified that Bishop had told her that he "fasted and prayed" before embarking on the affair and that "God had sanctioned the union."

The defense, of course, denied these charges and contended that the girl was older than sixteen, the legal age of consent. The defense also introduced testimony to "fix the crime" on another man, a "relative of the prosecutrix" and that it was easier to fix the blame on the preacher than on a member of the victim's family.

The preacher's wife, who was also reported as being an assistant to her husband in the church, sat by his side during the trial and had "frequent conferences" with her husband.

The newspapers reported that the public held intense interest in this case, following it from start to finish, and "the entire courthouse was occupied by white spectators, the 'Negroes' having been excluded from attendance by Judge J. Henry Johnson," wrote the *Watchman and Southron*. "The court room was packed and at times standing room was at a premium."

Murdaugh Sr. was highly successful in both public service and private practice. All the stars seemed to align for the rising southern lawyer. He was set to begin his sixth term as Fourteenth Circuit solicitor in January 1941.

"Grand Jury Lauds Murdaugh," a February 28, 1940, headline in the *Hampton County Guardian* read. "Endorsed for Re-Election."

But tragedy was bearing down at high speed on Murdaugh Sr. and his family.

The Associated Press reported that Murdaugh was leaving a late-night poker game around 1:00 a.m. on a Friday and his car stalled on the tracks. The *Hampton County Guardian*, his hometown paper, stated kindlier and simply that he was returning from a late visit with "friends in Yemassee," and there was no court session that day. Both reported that on July 19, 1940, Murdaugh Sr.'s car was crossing a railway about four miles east of Varnville when the car mysteriously stopped in the middle of the crossing.

A westbound Charleston and Western Carolina Railway freight train plunged ahead in the dark, steamy night. Murdaugh Sr. lifted his hand and waved at the oncoming locomotive, the driver later reported during an investigation.

The headlight beams drew closer and brighter, followed by the steaming, shaking rumble. Then the light, sound and speed overtook him.

Engineer W.W. Bartlett later testified that he did not see the car near the tracks until about forty yards away and that Murdaugh had his hand raised as though waving at the train crew. But when the train drew closer, the car started up and stopped directly on the tracks.

On July 24, 1940, the *Guardian* reported that "the impact hurled the automobile approximately 900 feet up the track, totally wrecking it," and "Murdaugh's body was found beside the track approximately 150 feet from the crossing."

Murdaugh Sr. had been suffering from health problems since 1939, the *Guardian* reported on several occasions, and had just been released from the hospital in April. Local historians have wondered if his health was a factor in this accident. Locals and historians have also wondered and speculated, without direct evidence, if alcohol was involved in this crash. Historical records and newspaper accounts give us no firm clue if that was the case. Others hint at suicide, again without probable cause.

Was the accident caused by railroad crossing conditions? Or were vehicle malfunctions to blame?

The Hampton County Coroner's jury simply ruled the death an accident. The public will likely never know the exact contributing cause of this collision, but the Murdaugh family had a suspicion, one that they would later take to court.

Within a week of the fatal 1940 train crash, the Fourteenth Circuit had a new solicitor. Randolph "Buster" Murdaugh Jr., who had trained at his father's side and worked as his assistant solicitor, was appointed to the office and would continue to grow the Murdaugh family legacy and fortune.

Murdaugh Jr. would start by taking legal revenge for his father's death.

Prior to his death, Murdaugh Sr. had taken on the railway company with lawsuits a time or two, but records do not suggest that this was a major focus of his practice. But that changed for the Murdaugh family and its law firm in the decades after his untimely death. Then, perhaps, it had become personal for the Murdaugh attorneys.

According to Hampton County Court of Common Pleas records, on October 1, 1940, Murdaugh Jr., as executor of his father's will and estate, filed a summons and complaint against the Charleston and Western Carolina Railway Company. The lawsuit brought action on behalf of his father's widow, Mary Murdaugh, and her children for the "wrongful death of said Randolph Murdaugh Sr."

The suit alleged that the train was traveling from Yemassee to Varnville "at a high rate of speed" and failed to blow a whistle or ring a bell at the Camp Branch crossing. The suit also alleged that the crossing and its approach "was in a rough, washed out and dangerous condition" and that Murdaugh's view was obscured by trees and tall underbrush on that foggy night, placing him in "sudden and imminent peril."

Murdaugh Jr. demanded a judgment of $100,000 for the death of his father. Court records filed on September 22, 1941, state that the case was settled. The amount was not disclosed.

The historic Charleston and Western Carolina freight line is an ancestor of modern-day CSX Transportation. In the century to come, CSX would become a favorite target of the Murdaugh law firm, so much so that locals would later refer to PMPED's towering law offices, one of the grandest buildings in Hampton County, as "CSX Towers" or "The House That CSX Built."

Historians can argue that this was the civil suit that started it all, the lawsuit that launched a legal legacy impacting people and businesses around the state and transforming the small, rural county of Hampton into what legal tort reformists would later call a "judicial hellhole."

RANDOLPH "BUSTER" MURDAUGH JR.

(January 9, 1915–February 5, 1998):
"The Cock of the Walk"

Buster Murdaugh's career can be described as a blend of greatness and alleged graft, of talent and alleged treachery. While ambition sums up the father's life, controversy captures the essence of the son's career.

While his father was known as either Randolph or Solicitor Murdaugh, the world would come to know his shorter, stockier son as "Buster," a name originally earned on the college gridiron but one that blossomed and assumed a whole new meaning in courts of law. You can learn much of what you need to know about Murdaugh Jr.'s personality from a brief encounter with the renowned Beaufort County novelist Pat Conroy, whose books about the

South Carolina Lowcountry earned numerous awards and inspired Oscar-nominated films.

In Conroy's 2013 memoir, *The Death of Santini: The Story of a Father and His Son*, he describes meeting Murdaugh Jr. in the Hampton County Courthouse during proceedings to get his job back on Daufuskie Island (an experience he also wrote about in *The Water Is Wide*). Conroy recalled an older man who sat in the jury box and "laughed his ass off" at several things the future novelist said during the trial. When the trial was over, Murdaugh Jr. called him over and introduced himself:

"I'm the cock of the walk in this part of South Carolina, and, boy, you really know how to put on a show," Murdaugh said before blowing cigar smoke in Conroy's face and asking him to give up teaching and come practice law with him. Buster even offered to send young Conroy to law school.

"I'll make you the goddamnedest lawyer you've ever seen," Murdaugh Jr. promised. The soon-to-be-famous author declined.

Murdaugh Jr. was a legend during his lifetime and after, and it was a colorful one, often of his own making. While his work ethic earned him "mountains of respect, tons of admirers," as one paper stated, it was the personality and flair of this southern lawyer that set him apart and made him a legal legend, albeit one filled with controversy. The courtroom was his stage, and he always put on a show, strutting the halls of justice and crowded courtrooms during tense murder trials with a signature wad of Red Man tobacco pinched in his cheek or a cigar in his mouth. He was known for his wit, especially in talking to the press, as well as his colorful courtroom theatrics and often flaming oratory. There is even an often-repeated Hampton County legend, unconfirmed but likely true, that when a circuit judge objected to his spitting tobacco juice in court, the solicitor packed up his files and left, effectively shutting the court down. They couldn't proceed without a prosecutor, and so the judge eventually relented.

During a 1956 Beaufort County murder trial, Murdaugh Jr. brought two hound dogs into the courtroom and entered them as evidence, quipping that he would not call on the hounds as witnesses if the defense would also "refrain from questioning them," later adding, "Defense and prosecution have agreed not to ask them more than three questions each." During a 1979 murder trial, he told a Beaufort County jury that he would never seek the death penalty again in that county if they didn't vote to execute. During the same trial, he splayed out on the floor in front of the jury box, playing the role of the victim. He asked a state's witness to tie an alleged murder weapon, a garden hose, around his neck, then questioned other defendants

A news clipping from the *Hampton County Guardian* depicting Randolph "Buster" Murdaugh Jr. *(far right)* at a crime scene. *Courtesy of the* Hampton County Guardian *archives.*

with the hose wrapped around his throat. He warned a jury once that if they did not deliver a guilty verdict in a Walterboro murder trial, they might as well put up a sign in blood on Interstate 95 that read, "Murderers Welcome in Colleton County." He told another Beaufort County jury that the suspect didn't think "y'all have got the guts to kill him."

Historians could argue that there was an amazing level of talent and greatness in Buster. Legal scholars could also argue otherwise, citing numerous violations of courtroom procedure and the rule of law. Murdaugh Jr. tended to play by his own rules in the courtroom, and once he earned a conviction or sent a man to death row, he cared little about appeals or overturned verdicts by a higher court.

Murdaugh Jr. was as powerful as he was talented and controversial. During more than four decades in both the civil and criminal courts of the Fourteenth Circuit and beyond, seizing on a stronghold established by two decades of service by his father, Murdaugh Jr. and his law firm developed a concentration of power. Murdaugh and his cronies had the power to place judges of law on the bench, including one attorney from their very own firm, Clyde Eltzroth. As an elected chief prosecutor for the circuit, Murdaugh Jr. knew how to work with people and developed a devoted following among voters, law enforcement officers and public officials alike. As a personal-injury lawyer, he took care of the "little guy" in high-dollar battles with massive companies and won hearts and minds in the civil courts in the process.

Even as Murdaugh Jr. prosecuted almost all major criminal cases in the five-county Fourteenth Circuit, either singlehandedly or later with his son Randolph Murdaugh III, he often stood accused of ethics and even criminal violations himself. Headlines around the state, from the 1940s well into the '60s, regaled readers with one accusation after another—but they never stuck. And every four years, voters would turn out in droves to reelect the popular prosecutor.

ACCUSATIONS A'PLENTY

Murdaugh Jr.'s controversaries began early in his career and would make headlines around the state. He was accused of everything from stealing cows and money from clients to cheating on his taxes and conspiring with moonshiners.

MURDAUGH THREATENED WITH DISBARMENT

In August 1949, the Hampton County Bar Association requested a "full, complete investigation" by the South Carolina Bar Association's Grievance Committee to determine if Murdaugh Jr. should be disbarred over allegations of breach of trust concerning a client—very similar to accusations that would later face his grandson Alex, albeit on a much smaller scale. The request came after a $50,000 civil suit was filed against Murdaugh Jr. by a former client. The breach of trust suit by J.V. McMillan alleged that Murdaugh failed to use money obtained as a mortgage to pay off one of the client's mortgages, adding that Murdaugh instead made monthly payments on the mortgages.

Murdaugh Jr. denied any wrongdoing and claimed the accusations were politically motivated. He told the papers that he would welcome an investigation to clear his name, adding, "It has always been my policy to fight my politics at the polls, but it would appear there are others who prefer to employ different means in such matters."

"I take it that those who wish to injure me want to try their case in the press," he added.

In October of that year, after what one newspaper described as a "secret" investigation and another a "secret hearing," the solicitor was cleared of all charges by the state's bar association.

After the hearing, Murdaugh Jr. filed a countersuit, saying that J.V. McMillan owed him $825.

"It is regrettable that the cost of this investigation, in the payment of witnesses expenses and the serving of subpoenas, will have to be borne by the taxpayers of Hampton County and I estimate it will run well over a thousand dollars," he told the press.

ALLEGATIONS OF TAX FRAUD

In 1955, Murdaugh Jr. was charged with tax fraud involving his legal fees by the federal government. Federal tax agents alleged that Murdaugh owed nearly $16,000 in additional taxes for the years 1945–48, plus more than $7,000 in penalties. The accused attorney appealed to the U.S. tax courts.

In September of that year, a U.S. tax court judge cleared him of those charges, citing both lack of proof and a statute of limitations, adding that the commissioner of the Internal Revenue Service failed to prove fraud.

This finding as to taxes owed, Judge Clarence V. Opper said in his opinion, "results to a considerable extent from the onus of the burden of proof which the petitioner Murdaugh found it impossible to rebut."

The court ruled that the alleged taxes due and penalties for 1945, amounting to about $14,099, were barred by the statute of limitations. Concerning the alleged fraud, Judge Opper wrote, "It may be that the petitioner was 'grossly negligent' in the keeping of records for tax purposes."

"So much he virtually concedes," the opinion added. "But however much his method of keeping records and assembling information for his tax returns left to be desired, carelessness is not synonymous with fraud."

WARRANT FOR LARCENY

In October 1968, Murdaugh Jr. was charged with "larceny after trust with fraudulent intent" in connection with a 1964 sawmill sale. The warrant was signed by L.J. Williams of Yemassee on behalf of his wife, who formerly owned Varnville Wood Products Company. The charges alleged that Murdaugh oversaw the title to the sawmill, which he sold for $22,000—$15,000 more than he had invested. But he allegedly kept the money for himself despite an agreement to split the profits equitably with his business partners.

THE PROSECUTION — Fourteenth Judicial Circuit Solicitor Randolph Murdaugh, Jr. (right) confers with his son, Assistant Solicitor Randolph Murdaugh, III during a break in the murder trial of Carl Pauls in Jasper County. (WAYNE ZURENDA PHOTO).

A news clipping from the *Guardian* depicting Randolph Murdaugh III (*left*) and his father, Buster Murdaugh, outside the Jasper County Courthouse during a break in a high-profile murder trial. *Courtesy of the* Hampton County Guardian *archives*.

After a three-hour hearing later that month, a Hampton County magistrate dismissed the charges, saying that there was insufficient cause.

In court, Williams produced a deed showing the sale of the sawmill to Hampton County Wood Products Inc. Murdaugh's attorneys, however, produced papers showing that a judgment had been placed against the Varnville sawmill for the sale amount, claiming that Murdaugh had never been paid. His attorneys went on to claim that since Murdaugh never got the money, he could not have "misappropriated" it.

THE GREAT COLLETON COUNTY WHISKEY CONSPIRACY

Of all the controversies surrounding Buster Murdaugh throughout the decades of his career, the most serious blemish on his career would take him all the way to federal court. The sweeping, scandalous affair would come to be called the "Great Colleton County Whiskey Conspiracy" and engulf local law enforcement, magistrates and the chief prosecutor.

The scandal was one "born in violence on a cold November morning," wrote the *State* in 1951. That's when federal agent Henderson Clary shot a bootlegger named Doc Freeman. Feds later learned of allegations that the wounded 'shiner was "in cahoots" with local law enforcement and court officials—and he didn't take too kindly to being shot by law-enforcement officers he thought were on his side.

On June 5, 1956, after a five-year investigation, Murdaugh Jr. was among a half-dozen defendants indicted by a federal grand jury in the state capital of Columbia for conspiracy to violate Internal Revenue laws relating to liquor. Several defendants had been indicted in Charleston the previous January, and the federal indictments, which eventually included a total of thirty defendants, alleged that in Colleton County, sometime after November 15, 1951, Murdaugh Jr. conspired with others to obtain from co-conspirator Edith Thigpen Freeman (who was not indicted) a notebook of incriminating notes made by co-conspirator D.B. "Doc" Freeman revealing protection money payoffs made by Mr. Freeman. He was also accused of conspiring to transport an illegal liquor distillery from Hampton County to Colleton County to prevent interference by local law enforcement. Specifically, investigators claimed that Murdaugh Jr. told bootlegger Robert F. Clifton to move his moonshine still into Colleton County to keep it away from a pending police raid.

Also indicted was Colleton County sheriff G. Haskell Thompson, who pleaded not guilty and sought legal assistance in keeping his job after the governor ousted him and appointed a replacement in the wake of the charges. Thompson refused to turn in his badge and obtained a state court injunction and "show cause" order in an appeal that went to the state supreme court. It was a futile attempt, however. The court denied his appeal, and Thompson lost his elected position anyway in the June 12 local Democratic primary.

On June 15, Murdaugh Jr. posted a $10,000 bond on the federal charges before U.S. Commissioner Gaines W. Smith. Murdaugh was arraigned on the charges on July 17, after twenty-eight of the other defendants had been arraigned. One defendant, Harry Richards, could not be located. The press reported that there was a delay in Murdaugh's arraignment because the solicitor had been busy prosecuting cases in state circuit court in Beaufort.

The case was scheduled for trial on September 17 in federal district court in Charleston.

In August, Murdaugh Jr.'s defense attorneys, Henry H. Edens and Henry Hammer, filed several motions seeking to have the charges dismissed on grounds of alleged improper grand jury evidence, and they alleged that prosecutors were promising "light sentences" to the other defendants to encourage testimony against Murdaugh. The motions requested that Murdaugh be tried separately from the other defendants, claiming that in a joint trial the solicitor could be found guilty "by transference" rather than by evidence. In the motions, Murdaugh's defense team added that, as solicitor, their client had prosecuted many of the co-conspirators and, if tried along with them, his "substantial rights to a fair trial will be prejudiced."

On August 20, following a pretrial conference, federal judge Walter E. Hoffman ordered federal prosecutors to turn over a list of all witnesses to Murdaugh's defense counsel and provide a list of documentary evidence. Judge Hoffman, who would also preside over the trial, denied Murdaugh's motions to dismiss the indictments altogether, denied the request for a separate trial and refused to strike out three "overt acts" in which Murdaugh was charged.

The release of the witness names—over strenuous objection by the federal prosecutors—would later prove problematic. According to a November 9, 1956 U.S. Department of Justice memo, this disclosure resulted in "very questionable practices on the part of some of the defendants and their attorneys during which government witnesses were threatened, attempts were made to influence them by promises of reward for themselves or members of their families and at least one attempt was made to intimidate or influence the United States Attorney."

On August 31, 1956, Murdaugh Jr. was struck with another charge: obstructing a Colleton County grand jury investigation of whiskey violations. The charges were filed in the U.S. District Clerk's Office in Charleston, along with a list of documents and evidence the federal government intended to use in its case against the accused solicitor. The new charges alleged that Murdaugh "attempted to prevent the jury from discovering whiskey violations by instructing former [Colleton County] Sheriff G. Haskell Thompson to make friendly raids upon known violators of Internal Revenue laws who at the time were paying for and receiving protection and advised them beforehand of the raids and assured them of protection in submitting to friendly prosecution."

The new charges also alleged that a defendant in the Colleton County whiskey conspiracy had commenced serving a prison term in 1951 for a federal whiskey violation to protect Murdaugh.

While the South Carolina governor removed one indicted public official—the Colleton sheriff—from office per state statute following the initial charges, he took no such action with Murdaugh. So unusual was this case, with Murdaugh remaining in office while being accused of federal crimes, that on September 5, the *Greenville News* ran the following headline: "Solicitor to Be Tried in One Court, Prosecute in Another Same Time."

General Sessions Court in Walterboro—in the same county in which Murdaugh stood accused, Colleton County—was slated to begin on September 17. When a prosecutor was unable to attend a court session, it was standard procedure for the South Carolina Attorney General's Office to appoint a solicitor from another circuit as a replacement, but Attorney General T.C. Callison told the *Greenville News* that he had not received a request to furnish a replacement for Murdaugh.

"Unless there is a change somewhere," wrote the *News*, "14th Circuit Sol. Randolph Murdaugh of Hampton will have to be in two courts at once Sept. 17; as prosecutor in one and defendant in the other."

On September 6, Murdaugh Jr. voluntarily resigned from the office of solicitor to devote all of his time to the preparation of his criminal defense and to defend his case at trial, which was originally expected to last up to six weeks. In his letter to South Carolina governor George Timmerman Jr., he stated that he was innocent of all charges, which were a "result of the activities of certain federal agents."

"The security, honor and happiness of my wife and children face destruction, my personal integrity and liberty are at stake," wrote Murdaugh Jr. The letter also expressed Murdaugh's "deep sadness" and appreciation for Timmerman's "confidence in my integrity," adding that he welcomed an "early opportunity" to clear his name of the "outrageous charges."

"With the help of Almighty God, the falsity of the charges will be bared and I will return to the office of Solicitor," Murdaugh Jr. concluded.

Timmerman accepted his resignation the same day and, the following day, appointed Beaufort attorney G.G. Dowling his interim replacement.

The Whiskey Conspiracy Trial

The opening day of the trial began with a surprise twist: one of the defendants, Colleton County deputy sheriff David Carter, changed his plea and admitted his guilt after the government's first witness took the stand and leveled some bombshell testimony. Thompson and Murdaugh Jr. maintained their innocence.

Edith Thigpen Freeman told the court that she had been keeping accounts of "payoffs" from bootleggers to former sheriff Thompson and former deputy Lucas Hiott. Freeman also testified about the disappearance of $13,000 from her house during a November 15, 1951, liquor raid during which her husband, alleged bootlegger and co-conspirator Doc Freeman, was shot. She alleged that deputies Hiott and Carter had searched the house and that the "bundle of money" was found to be missing afterward. She added that Hiott later gave her $500 and her husband $2,000.

During the second day of the trial, Edith Freeman offered more incriminating details, and a former federal agent backed up her story and placed the Colleton officers at the scene of the alleged liquor raid theft.

Malcolm Ewing, a retired Alcohol and Tobacco Tax Unit agent, recounted the raid on a 1,500-gallon liquor still located near the old Walterboro Air Base. He testified that Thompson, Hiott and Carter were at both the liquor still and the nearby Freeman house several times during the day of the raid.

In cross-examination by Murdaugh's defense team, Edith Freeman said that the money had been stolen from the pocket of a coat hanging in a closet at the Freeman home. "Actually, I do think Sheriff Thompson, Mr. Murdaugh and Lucas Hiott got the money, but I can't prove it," Freeman told Murdaugh's attorneys during questioning.

Also testifying that day were witnesses Alfred Moultrie and Joe T. Padgett, a former bootlegger turned commercial fisherman in Beaufort. Padgett admitted that he got into the "illicit whiskey business" in Colleton County in 1952. He testified that Colleton magistrate Berkeley C. Wood, also a defendant in the case, had introduced him to Sheriff Thompson. "Thompson asked me how much I could pay a month and I told him $200," Padgett told the court on the stand. "He told me to go ahead and get a location."

Padgett later told the court that the corrupt officials demanded twelve cases of whiskey a month—half for the sheriff and half for the magistrate—and testified about other payoffs. "Thompson told me if I could get $200— that was $100 for him and $100 for Mr. Murdaugh—that he would 'see what he could do' to get light probationary sentences" for two of Padgett's helpers who had been arrested.

During the opening days of the trial, another defendant, Robert A. McPeake, also pleaded guilty to get a reduced sentence.

The third day of the trial brought even more surprises and more innocent-to-guilty plea deals after tape-recorded evidence was introduced.

After the court heard from ten witnesses in the first two days, co-conspirator Robert Lee Varnadoe, charged with conspiracy and two counts of whiskey law violations, changed his plea to guilty. In exchange for the change of heart, Judge Hoffman dropped the two whiskey charges and accepted the plea to conspiracy. Hoffman deferred sentencing for Varnadoe until after the completion of the trial.

The federal government then introduced a tape recording as evidence, over the protests of the defense counsel. The recording was purported to be a conversation between Oscar Phillips, a local bootlegger, and Sheriff Thompson that was made on September 22, 1955, in the trunk of a car in which the men were sitting. While prosecutors had hoped the recording would be more of a major factor in their case, it did not catch the entire conversation, and much of it was "very indistinct and difficult to hear." The judge asked the jury to consider only the parts of the recording that could be understood and not to "speculate" on the rest.

The strongest testimony of the day came from co-conspirator Lucius Evans, who testified that he had made two separate whiskey still operation payoffs to two Colleton deputies and had paid another, Hiott, to retrieve a moonshine still condenser that had been seized as evidence in a raid.

As day three ended, the trial threatened to be a lengthy affair; federal prosecutors said they could call as many as one thousand witnesses and would be going into night and weekend sessions.

Toward the end of the first week of trial, former Colleton County deputy sheriff Ribbock Herndon testified that he gave Thompson $400 monthly in cash from retail stores and bootlegger payoffs. He also stated that any whiskey he received he would sell, then give the money to the former sheriff after deducting his own 20 percent. Even more shocking, Herndon told the court that he once gave Thompson four $100 bills from whiskey payouts while they were standing in the Colleton County Courthouse. He also said that, shortly afterward, he saw Thompson give Murdaugh Jr. two of the bills. Murdaugh Jr. reportedly got "very mad," because the money was exchanged in Herndon's presence.

The second week of the trial opened with more government witnesses talking of "friendly raids" on liquor stills and using paid informers and marked money to trace transactions, as Murdaugh's team prepared to launch its defense. Several bootleggers testified that they agreed to the friendly raids and entered guilty pleas in exchange for light fines to "help out" the officers with the grand jury and the citizens. There was even testimony by witnesses claiming they were paid to operate liquor stills for law-enforcement officers. By then, the list of defendants was down to twenty-one after charges were dismissed against four, four entered early guilty pleas and one defendant remained missing.

Murdaugh Jr. took the stand, and his questioning was described by the press as "a battle of wits and tempers" between the accused solicitor and Assistant U.S. Attorney Irvine Belser Jr. The "parry and thrust" game became heated at times. At one point, Judge Hoffman warned both sides and threatened Belser with contempt of court if the questioning again moved out of the agreed-upon "bounds."

The defense and the prosecution then brought forward witnesses who directly contradicted each other. The defense produced L.O. Browning, who testified that a bootlegger named Robert Clifton told him he intended to "get even" with Murdaugh Jr. for something. Clifton, a government witness, testified that he had never even met Browning and had never seen him before that day in court.

The defense then produced several character witnesses who testified in support of Murdaugh Jr., including Hampton County (Estill) grain elevator owner-operator Grover C. Bowers, who spoke of Murdaugh's "very good character."

In response to Bowers's raving endorsement, the feds introduced four character witnesses who testified against Murdaugh's "reputation for truth and veracity."

Final arguments began on September 28, and the matter was set to be turned over to the jury on Saturday, September 29. But faced with a Saturday-night session, the jury asked to wait until Monday to conclude the case and render its verdict. After the defense complained about newspaper coverage of the trail, Judge Hoffman urged the jurors to avoid reading any news reports over the weekend.

During the final arguments, the assistant district attorney described the indicted former public officials, including Murdaugh Jr., as "a bunch of buzzards and vultures." Murdaugh Jr. was again questioned at length by Belser about his alleged ties to the Colleton "whisky ring." In questioning, Belser drew from Murdaugh Jr. a statement that his law firm had once been paid $1,733 by one of the witnesses, Robert Clifton, for handling a whiskey case that went to the United States Supreme Court. That didn't sit well with the court or the judge.

Murdaugh defense attorney Claud N. Sapp then called the government's witnesses "a bunch of perjurers, thieves and convicts" and said the entire trial was an effort by these defendants to "get even" with Thompson and Murdaugh Jr. for having been harassed by law enforcement officials. At one point, Murdaugh's chief counsel, Edens, told the court, "I can write a better indictment for the government's witnesses than the government wrote for these defendants."

As the case reached its third week, Judge Hoffman advised the jury that it must reach a verdict or he would send them back repeatedly, adding, "This case is too complicated and lengthy to face a second hearing."

The jury's verdict came on Monday, October 1. Murdaugh Jr. and two other defendants were acquitted of all charges to join the four who had received early dismissals of charges. In addition to the five who had previously pled guilty, seventeen more defendants were convicted, including former sheriff Thompson; two of his deputies, including Hiott; and the former magistrate. One defendant, Harry Richards, was still missing or at large.

Judge Hoffman said that he would issue sentences the following day but warned all convicted law-enforcement officials that they would be receiving penitentiary sentences.

Sheriff Thompson earned the heaviest sentence: seven years in prison and a $3,000 fine. The deputies and magistrate received three years each, and the remaining defendants got two years or less.

In the final day of the session, as he was hearing pleas for leniency for the convicted, Judge Hoffman had a few strong words for the acquitted, including Murdaugh Jr. He described Murdaugh's conduct as "grossly unethical," including the fact that he represented accused bootleggers in other federal proceedings.

"I can't get involved in Colleton County politics, but I notice by the newspapers that Mr. Murdaugh plans to go back into office as solicitor," Judge Hoffman said in court. "He is an acquitted man and that is his prerogative. However, his unethical conduct—so grossly unethical by his own admission—was such that I couldn't go back and face my people if I were he. But that's his business and the business of the people there."

Neither Murdaugh Jr. nor his attorneys were in court that final day to hear these damning words, but Murdaugh Jr. later called it an "attack" and fired back in the press. "I feel it was unwarranted and entirely uncalled for in every respect," he said. "Because the judge's comments are privileged, having been made in open court, I have no recourse."

He added that representing bootleggers in federal court is a "standing practice" in this state and is authorized by South Carolina laws and had been for years.

"When the federal government sends a Republican judge into this state to tell South Carolinians how to handle their politics, it's a perfect example of the further encroachment by the government on the rights of the state."

A November 1956 U.S. Department of Justice memo on the case added further condemnation for Murdaugh Jr.:

The defense resorted to some highly questionable tactics, all apparently designed to bring about an acquittal or mistrial as to Solicitor Murdaugh even at the risk of sacrificing the remaining defendants. Strange incidents occurred during the trial, which sorely taxed the patience of the prosecutor. At one time one of the government's principal witnesses, after having testified previously in court, came to the United States Attorney, and told him that he had lied on the stand. Brought before the Court, however, he would admit only that his testimony had been erroneous in certain very immaterial respects which did not affect the issues in the case. Oddly enough, too, the foreman of the jury, immediately before the case was to go to the jury for deliberation, having received a telephone call informing him that his father was dying declined to accept the court's proffer of release, although an alternate juror was still present and available to take the foreman's place. It has been admitted by the foreman that he attended school with a brother of the defendant Murdaugh and in fact had dinner with him shortly before the trial began.

As result of this case, two obstruction of justice indictments have been returned and other allegations of misconduct with respect to the government's witnesses are under investigation.

Although acquitted, Solicitor Murdaugh was publicly castigated for his unethical practices by Judge Walter Hoffman....The Judge also felt it necessary publicly to call attention to the fact that it is a separate and distinct offense for anyone to threaten a person who has testified in court proceedings.

Federal officials could say what they wanted, but Buster Murdaugh owned the love and loyalty of too many hearts and minds—and votes—in the Fourteenth Circuit. Of course, his supporters were pleased with the verdict, including the Hampton grand jury. In an October 10, 1956, statement to the *Hampton County Guardian*, the grand jury stated, "We commend Randolph Murdaugh for the splendid manner in which he has handled the affairs of the office of solicitor. We deplore the outrageous charges brought against him and rejoice in his vindication. We sincerely hope he will return to the office of solicitor in the very near future and will continue to serve in that office as long as he desires."

On November 6, 1956, Murdaugh Jr. was swept back into office during general elections by a sizable majority in all five counties. On November 19, Governor Timmerman renamed him to his post as solicitor of the Fourteenth Circuit.

In early October, Alex G. Murdaugh, one of his first cousins from Orangeburg, South Carolina, had been indicted on charges of tampering with the federal grand jury. The indictments alleged that the Murdaugh relative attempted to influence a juror in the conspiracy case by telephoning Alfred R. Goodwin, the foreman of the jury, on September 13 or 14 to arrange a meeting at a nearby Florence, South Carolina restaurant. In December 1957, that Murdaugh was found innocent in federal court in Florence.

In the September 1957 term of Colleton County General Sessions, Murdaugh Jr. got revenge against two of the witnesses and co-conspirators who had testified against him in federal court in exchange for a lesser or dismissed charge. The solicitor pressed state charges against former deputy Riddick H. Herndon, a primary federal witness in the conspiracy trial, and former Jacksonboro district magistrate Herman M. Tuten, for violations of the state's liquor laws as part of the Colleton County whiskey ring—the same alleged crimes brought up in the federal trial. Both witnesses pled no contest to the charges.

Y'ALL THINK YOU CAN GET RID OF OL' BUSTER?

This oil painting of Randolph "Buster" Murdaugh Jr. hangs on an interior wall of the Hampton County Courthouse. *Courtesy of the* Hampton County Guardian *archives.*

Murdaugh Jr. was a prosecutor who convicted hundreds and sent at least nineteen to their deaths in the electric chair. But in an interview at his retirement, he told the *State* paper that his proudest moments were when he rehabilitated young people and changed their lives.

"Of all the things I'm proud of, it's helping young people get off that path that leads to criminality, that leads to the penitentiary," he said. "Putting people in the electric chair or getting them life in prison ain't no thrill at all."

Governor Dick Riley appointed Buster's son Randolph Murdaugh III to serve out the rest of Buster's unexpired term. But the elder Murdaugh stayed on part time to assist his son.

"So, if y'all think you can get rid of ol' Buster—you've got another think coming," Buster quipped.

His forty-six-year career as the Fourteenth Circuit solicitor (1940–86) is believed to be longest term of any solicitor in U.S. history.

RANDOLPH MURDAUGH III (OCTOBER 25, 1939–JUNE 10, 2021): THE MAN CALLED HANDSOME

Randolph Murdaugh III was just a few months old when his grandfather died in the 1940 train accident.

As a child, Murdaugh III often went to court with his father, serving as a jury boy picking numbers for jury selection at the age of eight and even visited crime scenes. For the most part, he was an eager pupil—but not in every case.

In April 1949, a horrible case shocked the rural community of Colleton County: an elderly farmer was accused of killing his older, semi-invalid siter and burying the body two feet deep in a pen where two hogs were kept.

At first, Wyman Hiott told deputies that he had found his sister, eighty-year-old Carrie Hiott Carter, dead and then disposed of the body in a rotting stable. Carter's body was found covered with fertilizer bags, blankets, fence posts and clay. But the farmer later confessed to police and to Buster

Murdaugh that he had poisoned his aged sister's coffee on April 5 and buried her—possibly alive—in the family hog pen. Murdaugh Jr. reported that Hiott admitted that he poisoned his sister "for pure meanness," because "she had messed her bed so many times."

The next day, Murdaugh Jr. said Hiott told him he dug a grave for her near a stable. Hiott was arrested on April 8, the day his sister's body was found in the barnyard grave behind their rural home. Murdaugh Jr. asked the local grand jury to indict Hiott for murder "by starvation, poisoning, or burying alive."

"I then went back to her bedroom, picked her up and placed her in the grave, covering her with blankets, then paper, then dirt. At that time, she was breathing a little," Hiott reportedly confessed to the solicitor.

Murdaugh III, only nine years old, was with his father at the time and heard the horrid details of the crime and heard the suspect's confession, he told the author during a 2018 interview.

The murder trial was set for June in the Colleton County Courthouse, and on the witness list, Solicitor Murdaugh included his son.

"You know you are going to have to tell the court what you heard," Buster told him, Randolph III recalled during the interview. "I didn't want to testify against the old man because he was sick and old, and I just felt sorry for both. I didn't want to be the one who put him away in prison for the rest of his life. But my father told me I was going to testify one way or another, even if he had to declare me a hostile witness."

Murdaugh III would nevertheless go on to follow in the footsteps of his father and grandfather. He served as Buster's assistant solicitor, then took the office on his father's retirement in 1986.

As solicitor, Murdaugh III tried more than two hundred murder cases—once earning two murder convictions in the same week—yet prided himself on knowing when a suspect deserved leniency or a second chance, he told his hometown paper, the *Hampton County Guardian*, in the 2018 interview. According to the family, Murdaugh III was instrumental in creating a pretrial intervention program in the Fourteenth Circuit to give first-time and young offenders a second chance.

Like his father, Murdaugh III had a smooth charisma that charmed juries and a sense of humor that endeared him to many. On the birth of his first granddaughter, he choose the nickname "Handsome," because "I always wanted a woman to call me handsome."

When a gentleman's strip club opened on Hilton Head Island and concerned citizens wanted action and tight regulations, he told a reporter

Solicitor Randolph Murdaugh III makes a speech from the balcony of the Hampton County Courthouse. *Courtesy of the* Hampton County Guardian *archives.*

that, for the good of the Fourteenth Circuit, he would "keep a close eye" on the club's activities. He was there on opening night, according to newspaper reports.

Murdaugh III would go on to earn the Order of the Palmetto, South Carolina's highest civilian honor bestowed by the state's governor, and the Murdaugh name would continue to be synonymous with legal power and public service in the Lowcountry as the family continued to amass land, wealth, privilege and prestige in multiple counties throughout the Lowcountry.

Murdaugh III served the public for almost twenty years as solicitor until he decided to go into private practice in 2006. His final term marked nearly eighty-six years that a Murdaugh served as the Fourteenth Circuit solicitor. But prosecution was in his blood, and he remained a part-time, paid assistant solicitor for years after his public retirement and was joined by his son Alex, who served as a volunteer, part-time assistant solicitor.

Murdaugh III died at his Almeda residence near Varnville on June 10, 2021, at the age of eighty-one—in the height of the criminal scandal surrounding his son Alex and just days after the shooting deaths of Maggie and Paul Murdaugh at their vast rural Colleton County estate, Moselle.

HOW WILL THE MURDAUGHS BE REMEMBERED?

For roughly a century, the Randolph Murdaughs donated to their communities, sent horrible people to prison or their deaths and helped scores of injured, grieving people in need through their private civil practice. Together, they earned almost every honor and accolade possible, including the Order of the Palmetto. Even the controversies and allegations surrounding the career of Buster Murdaugh could not ground the celebrated Murdaugh mystique or erase the love and loyalty that many people held for them.

But what took a century to build was destroyed in less than three years because of the unfortunate and tragic actions of Alex Murdaugh and his son Paul.

On Thursday, March 2, 2023, after a six-week trial in Walterboro, South Carolina, that incited an international media frenzy, Richard Alexander Murdaugh was convicted of both counts of murder in the shooting deaths of his wife, Margaret, and younger son, Paul. Prosecutors argued that Murdaugh, looking to hide other criminal acts, made the deaths look extraordinarily brutal, using multiple close-range gunshot wounds, in an effort to frame the killings as the work of angry vigilantes connected to the 2019 boat crash. The state also claimed that Murdaugh hoped the deaths would gain him sympathy and buy him some time to cover up his financial crimes.

But the Colleton County jury saw through the ruse, and the next day Murdaugh was sentenced to two consecutive life sentences in a maximum security prison.

With this tragic conclusion, the fall of the Murdaugh dynasty was complete. Today, only one of the Murdaugh descendants practices law in the family firm that no longer bears the Murdaugh name—it has been changed to Parker Law Group.

Now, with numerous lives ruined and communities shattered, the Murdaugh name will perhaps forever be tarnished in the eyes of millions.

FOR EVERY VILLAIN, A HERO

*A*uthor's note: Writing this book brought back many memories of stories and interviews that I had long forgotten. One of the stories that follow, "Hampton County's Lady Jailer," reminded me of this forgotten gem about the county's first female sheriff's deputy.

Several years ago, I had an opportunity to interview Blanche Winstead, who broke barriers for Hampton County's female deputies. Retired deputy Winstead shared the story of the Saturday night she arrested a prominent Estill lady who had enjoyed too much drink and gotten into an altercation. As the deputy reached for the cuffs, the woman pleaded with her.

"Please, you can't take me to jail!"

Dutybound, Deputy Winstead placed the cuffs on the lady despite the pleas.

"Please, I can't go to jail tonight!" the suspect persisted, struggling.

Winstead locked the shackles down firmly and pulled her toward the patrol car.

"You don't understand! I can't spend the night in jail! It's my turn to teach the Sunday School class Sunday morning!"

FOR EVERY VILLAIN, THERE should be a hero, a protagonist to challenge, thwart or overcome by sheer will the evil antagonist.

Not only is this the basic tenet in the mythical battle of good versus evil, but it is also one of the rules of storytelling. There must be crisis or conflict, but there must also be a hero, a character we can relate to, admire, pull for and perhaps seek to emulate to keep us interested and engaged in the story and make it more compelling.

In *Wicked Hampton County*, we have spent a great deal of time lurking about with the villains and their wicked deeds. But the darkness of the human spirit that is capable of so many terrible, heartless and cruel deeds can only be made right by the courage of those who dare try to stop it. The darkest part of humanity can bring out the light in the best of us. Sometimes, the worst of human behavior brings out the bravest and best of heroes.

In the case of the following stories, that bravery comes in the form of two kind ladies who dared to stand tall amid the evil men of their era.

Ripped from the Headlines

Hampton County Herald
January 25, 1916
Jailer's Daughter Holds Mob at Bay
Sadly, one of the bravest young souls in the county's pre-Depression era—a mere girl of fourteen—remains anonymous in the pages of history. Reports of her bravery were detailed in the *Hampton County Herald*, the *Hampton County Guardian* and even Charleston's *News and Courier*, yet none of them recorded the young lady's name.

Here is how the journalists of the day captured the event:

> *Dave Richards, a Black man from Estill, was taken from the county jail here last Saturday night by a party from Estill, and although not lynched, he was badly beaten up and left in the woods. According to the victim's statement, his life was spared as the result of the pleading of one member of the party defending the local jail.*
>
> *The reports of the affair vary, although the salient features are substantiated by a number of witnesses. The man, who was reportedly drunk, assaulted with a pistol a Mr. Glover, an elderly man, who clerks in the store of Marvin O'Neal at Estill. The suspect was arrested and taken to the jail at Estill.*
>
> *Later, the mayor of the town, upon learning that a party was being formed to take the man from the jail and lynch him, had him removed by*

automobile to the county jail at Hampton. Magistrate Constable J.A. Cook and John O. Smith brought him to Hampton.

Crowd Makes for the Door

Arriving at the county jail, the jailer, J.P. Bowers, proceeded upstairs to the cells with the prisoner, locking the front door of the jail. Then one of the men who brought the man to Hampton went back downstairs to fetch the man's hat, which he had dropped in a failed escape attempt. When the constable unlocked the door and exited, he was met by a party of about 35 men, according to his estimation, who rushed for the open door.

Just as the crowd reached the door, the jailer's daughter, who is about 14 years of age, ran into an adjoining room, grabbed one of her father's pistols, and rushed back to the angry mob, covering the lynching party with the revolver, and declaring that she would shoot the first one that entered the door.

She held them at bay until her brother, fearing that some harm might overtake her, took the pistol from her, whereupon some of the crowd rushed in and went upstairs, overpowered the jailer, took the prisoner and fled in automobiles in the direction of Estill.

Sheriff Notified

Her brave actions not over, the young lady then notified Sheriff Lightsey by telephone that the prisoner had been taken away by five or six men. She stated that it was a "put up" game. The Sheriff left Brunson, where he resides, for Hampton and immediately took up the trail of the party but was unable to find out anything as to their whereabouts of the mob or its intended victim. Jailer Bowers pleaded with the party not to lynch the man, after they had overpowered him and taken his prisoner.

Today, the man was found at a friend's house a few miles from Hampton. He seemed to be still drunk and was badly beaten. The theory is, in addition to the pleadings of the jailer and his daughter, that the would-be lynching party feared they would be easily recognized and prosecuted if they killed their victim. Several members of the Estill mob were recognized by several people in Hampton, as cars from Hampton were following the party closely, so the would-be lynch mob decided not to kill the man but beat him and throw him out of the car.

Richards was given medical attention and brought back to Hampton to await trial. Later, he was removed from the jail and taken, presumably, to Columbia for safekeeping. It was stated that indictments will be issued for the members of the party, particularly all of whom were recognized, and their prosecution will be pressed vigorously. None of them wore a mask.

County Jailer Reveals More of the Story

Upon reading the account of the affair in The News and Courier, *the jailer, J.P. Bowers, stated to* The Courier's *correspondent that the prisoner was never delivered over to him properly; that the man was not truly in his custody, for the reason that the constable "had no commitment." He stated that the man was brought to the jail by constables J.A. Cook and John O. Smith of Estill. Bowers added that these two men left the prisoner with him on the stairs leading to the cells, and then one of the men went to the front door of the jail, unlocked it, threw it open, and said to the lynching party on the outside; "Come on in, fellows, and get him."*

It was noted that the members of the party are prominent in Estill.

July 19, 1972

Hampton County's Lady Jailer

A Hampton widow, 64 years old, has an occupation that is decidedly different. It is a safe bet she is one of only a very small number of lady jailers in the state and nation.

Mrs. W.L. Woods, whose snow-white hair catches the eye, became a custodian of the Hampton County Jail in the county seat in 1952. At that time, her husband, W. Lee Woods, jailer for the county, had just died after a period of ill health. Mrs. Woods has done a bang-up job and Hampton County officials and law enforcement officers of the county and state have found her entirely satisfactory for the post and are pleased with her record. She had no means of livelihood and was at a loss when her husband died, so she was eager to accept the job and has not regretted it.

Mrs. Woods and her daughter, Elizabeth, lived downstairs while there are between five to 15 prisoners for a wide variety of crimes. Since the local jail was a "trouble hub" for the county law enforcement, in addition to caring for the prisoners Woods gets on the shortwave radio and serves as the county dispatcher at night.

In 1952, sixty-four-year-old W.L. Woods became custodian of the Hampton County Jail and the first female jailer in county history. *Courtesy of the* Hampton County Guardian *archives.*

There has been only one jailbreak and another attempted since she took over the keys. The county's boarders have been kept in orderly fashion for the most part. The jail has been kept clean. Flowers grow in the yard and in porch boxes. There is a vegetable garden, chickens in the back yard and pet cats lounging on the front steps. Prisoners have not found much to complain of and at mealtime they fare better than in most jails. They even get a hot supper on Sunday nights.

Mrs. Woods does many extra things for prisoners, often going out of her way to do considerate things, giving motherly attention to the young boys on a wayward track and far from home and family.

In the six years she has served as jailer, Mrs. Woods says, only rarely has a prisoner been disrespectful. She treats the men behind bars as human beings, with kindness and sympathy. They, in turn, seldom cause her inconvenience or trouble. She is able to sleep just as peacefully in her jail apartment downstairs as if in her own home. She has never feared the prisoners, nor has it upset her to have a murderer locked in upstairs for weeks at a time.

She feels that the saddest of all sad experiences is that of locking up a youth for any period of time. She has never become hardened to it, depriving a teenager of his liberty for some infraction of the law. "It is tragic for me every time it happens, and I feel heartsick when young people are brought in for keeping," she explained.

Because she is unusually kind and understanding in her manner of handling prisoners, many of them who have returned to normal lives after their troubles were settled and their debt to society paid have come back to call on the kindly white-haired jailer of Hampton. They have phoned and written on occasions to report a successful rehabilitation. They long remember the kind manner in which they were treated while behind bars.

Hampton County's lady jailer will never forget one of the first prisoners she had to lock up. None since has appealed to her sympathy quite so much. He was a schoolboy, less than 15 years old, who killed his mother and father. From the time of the tragedy until the time of his trial, the boy was kept in jail and is now serving his sentence in the state penitentiary. Sisters of the schoolboy still remind Mrs. Woods of their appreciation for her goodness to him while in her care.

Several times she has put a small stake on a prisoner's future by placing a bill in his hand as he left penniless after serving a long jail sentence. She has found warm clothing for another prisoner who came in summer and left in winter without warm clothes and a flat wallet.

Dealing with the deep troubles of others has helped her adjust to a life of widowhood. "I buried my own troubles in the troubles of others," Mrs. Woods said. "I have spent my spare time in jail keeping by trying to do small things to help troubled prisoners."

MODERN-DAY
HAMPTON COUNTY

There are places like Hampton County scattered across small-town America, and like those locales, our county has seen much change over the centuries.

Hampton County's population has shrunk over the last one hundred years or so, but the souls who remain are, as a whole, kinder and gentler.

As a historian and my hometown's newspaper editor for two decades, I have seen the worst wickedness that this rural, southern place is capable of. But I have also seen Hampton County at its best.

When a historic, record-breaking tornado ravaged our county in a blitzkrieg of catastrophe in April 2020, leaving five people dead, I witnessed firsthand the citizens of this county rushing out to help neighbor and stranger alike. I have seen these people rally to aid others in all forms of peril, from natural disasters and catastrophic accidents to disease and death, all to the rally cry of "Hampton County Strong."

On July 1, 2021, the county's two public school districts, one still composed of mostly underserved minority students, officially consolidated into one new entity, the Hampton County School District. North and south have finally merged, and "both sides of the swamp," once divided by geography, race and economics, are gradually coming together for the first time in our history. There are even plans to build one comprehensive, consolidated high school near the center of the county. This is an important, symbolic step in our county and its efforts to bring our people together, finally erasing our geographic, racial and cultural divides.

If history has taught us anything, it is that change is inevitable. Change is underway in this place I call home, and it will continue to change—hopefully for the better.

There is history here in Hampton County, and indeed, much of it was wicked. But there is also hope here, and brotherly love and a desire to grow and change, and that should be the story of our children's future.

BIBLIOGRAPHY

Chapter 1. Hampton County's First Families

Bache, Ben. *South Carolina: Great Stories That Embrace the History of the Palmetto State*. Greenville, SC: Homecourt Publishers, 2005.

Encyclopedia Britannica. "Yamasee War." www.britannica.com.

Hampton County Guardian. "Hampton County by 4 Names, Under 4 Flags." June 21, 1978.

Hampton County Museum publications. Hampton County Historical Society. Hampton County, South Carolina.

Hampton, South Carolina. "Historical Profile of Hampton County." www.hamptoncountysc.orgy.

Morris, Michael P. "Yamasee War." *South Carolina Encyclopedia*. Originally published July 7, 2016; updated August 22, 2022. www.scencyclopedia.org.

Parker, Jay. "Indian Facts: Indians in Hampton County and Surrounding Areas." Hampton Museum and Visitors' Center, 1997.

Chapter 2. Rebels and Red Shirts

Bache, Ben. *South Carolina: Great Stories That Embrace the History of the Palmetto State*. Greenville, SC: Homecourt Publishers, 2005.

Beaufort County. "About Beaufort County." www.beaufortcountysc.gov.

Hampton County Guardian archives, 1879–present.

Hampton County Tricentennial Commission. *Both Sides of the Swamp: Hampton County*. Hampton County Historical Society, 1970.

Chapter 3. Wade Hampton and the Riot of 1880

Hampton County Guardian archives, 1879–present.

Hampton County Guardian. "125 Years, 1879–2004: Hampton County's History as Recorded on the Pages of *The Hampton County Guardian*." 125th anniversary edition, September 30, 2004.

University of South Carolina. "Appendix 11: Research Reports on Building Names–Wade Hampton College." University History. https://sc.edu.

Chapter 4. Moonshine, Sue Cat and Other Demon Brews

Bache, Ben. *South Carolina: Great Stories That Embrace the History of the Palmetto State*. Greenville, SC: Homecourt Publishers, 2005.

Gillespie, Bob. "Moonshine and Its 'Kin' Now Part of South Carolina Tourism Scene." Discover South Carolina. https://discoversouthcarolina.com.

Hampton County Guardian archives, 1879–present.

Moss, Robert F. *Southern Spirits: Four Hundred Years of Drinking in the American South, With Recipes*. Berkeley, CA: Ten Speed Press, 2016.

Smith, Fleming. "SC's Moonshine Culture and Its Long, Bullet-Riddled History." *Post and Courier*, January 10, 2020.

Smith, Kathryn. *Baptists and Bootleggers: A Prohibition Expedition through the South*. Charleston, SC: Evening Post Books, 2022.

Chapter 5. Unholy Deeds

Hampton County Guardian archives, 1879–present.

Hampton County Guardian. "125 Years, 1879–2004: Hampton County's History as Recorded on the Pages of *The Hampton County Guardian*." 125th anniversary edition, September 30, 2004.

Chapter 6. Sticky Palms and the Five-Finger Discount

Hampton County Guardian archives, 1879–present.

Hampton County Guardian. "125 Years, 1879–2004: Hampton County's History as Recorded on the Pages of *The Hampton County Guardian.*" 125th anniversary edition, September 30, 2004.

Chapter 7. "Wild East" Outlaws

Gibson, Dawn Bowden. Interview with Michael DeWitt Jr. "Salkehatchie Stew," July 9, 2010.

Gordon, Sara Janna. "History of the Town of Hampton Courthouse." Hampton Museum and Visitors' Center, 2004.

Hampton Museum and Visitors' Center. "Legends and Stories of the Town of Hampton." 2004.

South Carolina House of Representatives Resolution (H. 4244) to Commemorate Palmetto State Bank Centennial, 2007.

Chapter 8. Mysterious Diseases and Deaths

Hampton County Guardian archives, 1879–present.

Hampton County Guardian. "125 Years, 1879–2004: Hampton County's History as Recorded on the Pages of *The Hampton County Guardian.*" 125th anniversary edition, September 30, 2004.

Hampton Museum and Visitors' Center. "Legends and Stories of the Town of Hampton." 2004.

National Library of Medicine. "Pellagra." National Center for Biotechnology Information. September 2015. https://pubmed.ncbi.nlm.nih.gov.

Peeples-Rhoden Funeral Home. "Who We Are: Our Story." https://www.peeplesrhodenfuneralhome.com.

Reynolds-Finley Historical Library. "History of Pellagra." The University of Alabama at Birmingham. https://library.uab.edu.

Chapter 9. Wickedness at the Old Jail

Hampton County Guardian archives, 1879–present.

Hampton County Guardian. "125 Years, 1879–2004: Hampton County's History as Recorded on the Pages of *The Hampton County Guardian*." 125th anniversary edition, September 30, 2004.

Hampton County Historical Society. "The Old Hampton County Jail." hchssc.org.

South Carolina Humanities. "Video about The Hampton County Old Jail." schumanities.org.

Chapter 10. Racism, Civil Rights and the Confederate Legacy

Hampton County Guardian archives, 1879–present.

Hampton County Guardian. "125 Years, 1879–2004: Hampton County's History as Recorded on the Pages of *The Hampton County Guardian*." 125th anniversary edition, September 30, 2004.

Hampton County Tricentennial Commission. *Both Sides of the Swamp: Hampton County*. Hampton County Historical Society, 1970.

McInerney, Peter. "A Call to Justice—Hampton County, South Carolina." *The University of Notre Dame Class of 1969 Blog*, 1969. www.notredameclassof1969blog.blogspot.com.

———. "The Good, the Bad, and the Ugly in Hampton County." *Scholastic Magazine*, May 3, 1968.

Town of Brunson. "History." www.brunson.sc.gov.

Chapter 11. Grisly Murders Stain the Pages of History

Hampton County Democrat. March 2, 1951; March 30, 1951; June 7, 1951.

Hampton County Guardian archives, 1879–present.

Hampton County Guardian. "125 Years, 1879–2004: Hampton County's History as Recorded on the Pages of *The Hampton County Guardian*." 125th anniversary edition, September 30, 2004.

The State (Columbia, SC), September 13, 1928, 6.

Chapter 12. Moonshine, Murder and Murdaugh Mayhem

DeWitt, Michael M., Jr. *Fall of the House of Murdaugh: The Rise and Fall of a South Carolina Legal Dynasty*. Charleston, SC: Evening Post Books, 2023.

Hampton County Guardian. "125 Years, 1879–2004: Hampton County's History as Recorded on the Pages of *The Hampton County Guardian.*" 125th anniversary edition, September 30, 2004.

Hampton County Guardian archives, 1879–present.

Hampton County Historical Society. *From the Salkehatchie to the Savannah: A Visual Journey through Hampton County.* 2006.

Williams, Rose-Marie Eltzroth. *Railroads and Sawmills: Varnville, S.C. 1872–1997; The Making of a Low Country Town in the New South.* Varnville, SC: Varnville Community Council, 1998.

Chapter 13. For Every Villian, a Hero

Hampton County Guardian archives, 1879–present.

Hampton County Guardian. "125 Years, 1879–2004: Hampton County's History as Recorded on the Pages of *The Hampton County Guardian.*" 125th anniversary edition, September 30, 2004.

Chapter 14. Modern-Day Hampton County

Hampton County Guardian archives, 1879–present.

INDEX

ABOUT THE AUTHOR

*H*ampton County native Michael M. DeWitt Jr. is a multiple-award-winning journalist and longtime editor of the 143-year-old *Hampton County Guardian*. DeWitt's boots-on-the-ground coverage of the Murdaugh crime saga has been published in print and online in Gannett's nationwide USA TODAY Network, and he has appeared on ABC's *20/20*, CBS's *48 Hours*, *Dateline NBC* and Netflix documentaries to discuss the case.

As a humorist, DeWitt's award-winning southern humor newspaper column, "Southern Voices, Southern Stories," was published in newspapers from Cape Cod to Northern California, and he has been a regular contributor to *South Carolina Wildlife* magazine, *Sporting Classics* magazine and its online counterpart, *Sporting Classics Daily*.

For four years, DeWitt served as volunteer historian, storyteller and playwright for the five-county "Salkehatchie Stew" oral history and community theater project sponsored by the University of South Carolina. In 2014, he was named the Hampton County Chamber of Commerce's Person of the Year for his service to the community.

DeWitt is also the author of Images of America: *Hampton County* (Arcadia Publishing/The History Press, 2015), a photo history of the place his family has called home for close to three hundred years.